MOMMA'S
BLACK REFRIGERATOR

A Memoir

Florence Tannen

9/11/17

To Myra,

never give up on your dreams

Library of Congress Cataloging-in-Publication Data
Names: Tannen, Florence, author.
Title: Momma's black refrigerator : a memoir / Florence Tannen.
Description: First American edition. | Albuquerque, NM : Casa de Snapdragon
   LLC, 2017.
Identifiers: LCCN 2017023749| ISBN 9781937240851 (pbk.) | ISBN 9781937240875   (epub)
Subjects: LCSH: Tannen, Florence--Family. | Mothers and daughters--Biography. | Familes of the mentally ill--Biography. | Life change events.
Classification: LCC PS3620.A6864 Z46 2017 | DDC 818/.603--dc23 LC record available at https://lccn.loc.gov/2017023749

20170722
Casa de Snapdragon LLC
12901 Bryce Avenue, NE
Albuquerque, NM 87112
casadesnapdragon.com

Printed in the United States of America

With love to my husband Jules, who always encouraged me to get this story told and never doubted my ability to do it.

"I'm so glad you're here, Flori."

"What's wrong, Momma? You seem upset."

"I'm afraid of the big storm that's coming."

"But, Momma, the sun is shining."

"I know, but look at the wind whipping the trees around. What happens if the rains come and the oceans fill up so much they reach the sky?" she asked.

"It's going to be okay."

"But, the oceans would press against the universe and the pressure could make the sky fall. It could fall and knock down buildings and bring them crashing down on our heads."

"See, Momma, the sun is shining and the wind stopped blowing."

She looked at the window with a worried expression on her face. "Are you sure it's okay out there?"

"It's fine."

Momma is dressed in a creased flowered cotton housedress buttoned down the front with tissues sticking out of her pocket. She is wearing white cotton anklets and gray shoes. Her hair is white, thin, and brushed back from her face, which is now covered with many brown spots. Her chin is sprouting lots of curly white hairs.

"What's that you have in that bag? Bananas! Oh God bless you. My favorite food. Mmm! Now that's delicious," she said as she took one from the bunch, quickly peeled the skin back, and bit off a piece. "What would I do without you? No one else worries because they weren't given the power to see like me. I was so scared before."

"I'm here now, Momma."

"Isn't it wonderful that you – my own daughter – came to visit me on this very day? I've been sitting here praying to the Good God Above and see – he sent me you – to bring me bananas – to tell me not to worry. Thank God. I was so afraid they'd get to you."

How many years have I visited her? First in Creedmoor State Hospital where they took her when I was nine and a half, and later as a teenager, a married woman, a mother of my own children. How many years? First thinking she was fine, and not understanding why she was there. And gradually hearing more and more of this kind of talk. Was she okay when she left? Maybe I heard and didn't want to believe it. Maybe she got crazy being in the hospital all these years. Maybe they did it to her with their medications—the shock treatments—maybe?

What difference does it make? She's old now – living in a nursing home. She is just suffering from dementia, and loss of memory, like other old people. No one even has to know about the years of being locked away and never coming home. Why can't I let it go?

Because, no matter how much I've heard, there is so much I don't know. So much I want her to tell me.

But, when she talks like this, how much can I believe? I want to scream at her, Please stop it, Momma, you're scaring me, but I don't. My head is pounding, my stomach is in knots, and I want her to stop, yet – I don't – so I let her go on.

"Listen, you have to hear this. It's what I've learned from living here. You're my daughter and you should know too. Sometimes they try to reach me from the television, but I turn it off. The fighters come and get jobs here. You didn't know that, did you?"

"No, Momma, I didn't."

"They put something in the food here. Something to torture my mind. Today they made me more intelligent to see what's going to happen to the universe. THAT'S how they torture my mind, by making me worry!"

"Why would they do that to you, Momma?"

"Because – they're jealous!"

"What are they jealous of?"

"They think – that I think – that I'm superior to them – so they get angry and resentful and they want to fight. Don't be upset, Flori, the Good God Above sends me lots of good ones to fight off the fighters so they can't do any damage."

In the past, when I visited with Momma, we always played the game, "Remember." I asked lots of questions and she tried to remember. Questions like—

'How old are you? When's my birthday? When's Lillian's? Do you remember the apartment on the fourth floor, or the black refrigerator?'

We'd repeat these question and answer periods over and over at least four or five times. Each time would be as if I'd just come through the door. Sometimes she'd remember the answers and sometimes she couldn't. And, sometimes she'd tell me of scenes that happened before I was born, which I'd listen to hungrily, hoping to fill in some of the pieces that no one else remembers. But, I never stopped trying to bring her back to the place I can't forget.

"Remember, Ma. The yellow table?"

"Where?"

"In our apartment on Carroll Street."

"I never lived there."

"How old are you, Ma?"

"I was born in 1908, you figure it out."

"You're ninety-one years old."

"Really? I don't feel that old. How do I look?"

"You look beautiful, Ma." I say, and her whole face lights up.

"You look beautiful, too, Flori."

"That's because I look just like my mother."

I look at my watch; it's getting late. There is no time left today to play our game. I put my coat on.

"Where are you going?"

"Home, Ma. I have to make supper for my husband."

"Of course, Sweetiepuss. Give him my regards. And, don't forget; send my love to the boys too."

Momma stands up, wraps her arms around me and gives me a hug. I hug and kiss her too.

I leave her room and turn back to look at her. She

is very busy listening to the voices that only she can hear.

"You can't get to me now. I told you. I'm not alone. I have mine," she says as she makes a fist and points it at the ceiling.

As I wait for the elevator, I shake my head. It feels like a big box that I constantly dig into, filled with loops of old film that I need to sort out. When I hold them up to the light, I see scenes. Scenes in Brooklyn, in the Forties. Momma and I used to watch these scenes together, but the ones in her head are getting dimmer. A lot of the fragments have been destroyed. Lately, she tells me about scenes that I'm not a part of.

I am obsessed with splicing together the clips I have before they fade, or I lose them altogether. It's my life, but I feel like I'm watching it happen to somebody else. I'm watching them all – Momma, Daddy, Lillian and me, little Flori.

ONE

LOSING FLORI

"Tell me again, Daddy. Tell me that story, please!"

Daddy picked me up and held me close, tickling my neck with his nose. I hugged him tight, smelling the scent of lavender Sen-Sen that Daddy was always sucking on. I didn't like the taste of those tiny little black squares, but Daddy said they made his breath smell good.

"Well..." he hesitated, like it was hard to remember, and then, with a twinkle in his green eyes, continued.

"It was a hot summer, and we rented a place in Brighton Beach."

"Did we go swimming there?"

"That's why we went there so Momma could take you swimming every day. Now let's see...Lillian was outside playing with her friends. Momma gave you your bath, put you in your pajamas."

"And tucked me in my bed."

Daddy hugged me tighter and tried to kiss my nose. I wriggled in his arms.

"Don't, Daddy. Your whiskers scratch." He kissed my hair as I settled in his lap. "Did it happen then, Daddy?"

"Momma changed into a pretty blouse and a pair of cotton slacks, and combed her hair. Then..."

"After she combed her hair, Momma put on her red lipstick, Daddy."

Daddy smiled. "Yes – her red lipstick. Now where

was I? Oh yes. When Momma was sure you were asleep, she joined the neighbors sitting outside on the stoop..."

"Or on folding chairs?"

Daddy nodded.

"What did they do there?"

"They talked about the day, their children, shopping, and the weather – things neighbors talk to each other about."

He put me down, walked over to the sink, and poured himself a glass of water.

"What happened next?" I asked, as if I hadn't heard this story a hundred times before.

"Oh nothing. They just kept on talking."

"Daddy!"

"Okay. I came home from work, and went inside to eat my supper and change my clothes. I walked into your room to see if you were sleeping."

"It was dark in there."

"Yes it was, so I left the door open and the light from the hall was enough for me to see. That's when it happened." He put his hand to his face and opened his mouth and eyes as wide as he could. I put my hand to my face, but as hard as I tried I couldn't open my eyes and mouth as wide as Daddy did.

"I looked in the bed, and – you know what?"

"What, Daddy?"

"You weren't there!"

"What did you do?"

"I checked one side of the bed and then the other. I pulled back the covers and I inspected every inch of the bed. I even got my flashlight and bent down to see under the bed. I thought, maybe my Flori rolled down there. I was sooo worried. I didn't know where my little girl was."

"Were you scared, Daddy?"

"I was never more scared in my life, but I didn't give up! I looked in every corner of the room. First I looked in the corner where you left your Betsy-Wetsy doll. Then I went to the corner where you set the table for tea, and then to where your paper dolls were sleeping, and then... "

I held my breath. This was my favorite part.

"I smelled something funny." Daddy squeezed his nose with his fingers.

"Yuk," I said squeezing mine.

"I followed the smell and it led me to the white wicker chair where Momma had laid out my pants. And guess what?"

"What, Daddy?"

"I found my Flori, sitting on the chair with her pajama pants pulled down. She was sound asleep. Do you know what she had done?"

"What?"

"She must have had to go to the bathroom, and in her sleep thought the chair was the toilet. She sat down, and peed all over my best pants."

I laughed, and Daddy laughed. He put me on his shoulders, and carried me all around the room.

TWO

THE OTHER SIDE

"Come on, Flori, you have to finish your bath. It's time for bed. Stop that! You're getting water all over everything." Momma was smiling. I knew Momma wasn't really angry, so I kept on splashing.

"Okay, that's enough."

I could tell from the look in Momma's eyes, that now she meant it. Reluctantly, I stepped out of the tub. Momma wrapped me in a large, bright, white towel, dried me all over, helped me into my pajamas, and gave me a big hug. I wrapped my arms and legs around her.

"Carry me, please! Carry me to bed."

"Flori, you're getting too heavy to be carried."

"Please, Momma, please. Carry me," I begged, tightening my arms and legs.

"I can't, I have this pain in my hip."

Momma pointed to her left side. She never had a pain before. I let go immediately and ran into the bedroom that I shared with my older sister.

"Lillian, Lillian," I cried, "Momma has a pain. Momma, show her."

I turned around. Momma was showing Lillian the place where it hurt, but this time she was pointing to the other side.

THREE

SKIPPING TO THE LIBRARY

Momma and I walked up to the big stone steps that took us into the Grand Army Plaza Library. She showed me where she would be sitting and reading while she waited for me. Then she walked me down the hall to the room where all the other children were.

The sunny yellow room had bright red and royal blue chairs that were just the right size. The colors reminded me of my crayons at home.

Pictures of boys and girls with books were on the wall. In the pictures, children were sitting on little wooden chairs, listening to someone read to them, just like I was doing. One of the things I liked best was to listen to stories being read aloud. It didn't matter if it was Momma reading to me from *Alice in Wonderland,* or I heard them on radio programs like *Mr. First Nighter* or *Let's Pretend,* or here in the library. I loved them all.

I was happiest when I picked out books to take home. I could read them over and over and didn't have to bring them back until the following week when it was reading time at the library again. I brought home *Black Beauty* and *The Five Little Peppers and How They Grew.* These were two of my favorites. *A Secret Garden* was another.

Each week I found more favorites. There were so many books I wanted to read but I could only take two at a time. Momma enjoyed the stories as much as I did and I would read them aloud to her as she cooked, cleaned and washed our clothes.

Momma and I always walked to the library from our apartment. One day, she turned to me, gave me a big smile, and started to skip. I began to skip too.

We laughed and skipped all the way there. I was so happy; I thought my heart would burst.

FOUR

BLANKETS AND TEARS

Momma decided it was time for us to have new furniture in our bedroom.

So we all went shopping on Rockaway Avenue.

We looked and looked, but nothing pleased her.

"Enough already, Blanche. We're all getting tired. We've seen lots of nice bedroom suites. Pick one, and let's go home."

"One more store, Abe. Come on, girls. Just one more store."

At the next store, Momma rushed through the showroom ahead of us, looking at one set, and on to another.

"Over here. Take a look at this," she yelled.

Momma was stroking a dresser made of blond wood. The headboards of the twin beds, the dresser fronts, and the wooden frame of the mirror had painted scenes of cactus with Mexicans next to them, sleeping under their big sombreros.

"You have excellent taste," the salesman said. "This is one of our finest sets, from the Monterey Line."

"It'll be perfect for my girls."

"It's too expensive, Blanche. Forget it."

Eventually he gave in, and the bedroom suite was delivered to our apartment. Momma ran her hands lovingly over each piece.

Now that we had new beds, she wanted new blankets. Daddy said there was nothing wrong with our blankets, and besides, he couldn't afford new ones. When Momma's blankets were "stolen" from the clothesline, what could Daddy do? A family had to have blankets.

Momma and I took the subway to Manhattan to shop at Macy's. We went to the Linen Department where she looked at the sheets, pillows, curtains, and finally at the blankets. When she picked out the ones she liked, she found a saleslady who took her money and packed up the blankets for us to take home.

We took the escalator down, crossed the street, and walked upstairs to the Chinese restaurant. Momma dropped her heavy package on the leather booth and sat down next to it. I sat opposite her. We looked out the window and watched the people down below.

In front of each of us, the waiter placed a fork, two teaspoons, three soup spoons, a white linen napkin, and a glass of water with ice

Momma ordered two egg drop soups, one order of eggrolls, and one order of chicken chow mein. The waiter brought us hot tea in a metal teapot and two blue and white small cups without handles or saucers.

Momma poured us each a cup of tea. I watched the tea leaves swirl around the brown liquid and eventually settle on the bottom of our cups. Momma and I opened the divided metal top of the glass bowl, took out lumps of sugar, and plopped them into our tea cups. We stirred the tea, until the tea leaves settled again. Delicately, with her pinkie raised, she took the first sip.

"Ah," she said, as she smacked her lips, "That's good!" I did the same.

When the hot soup arrived, Momma took the fried noodles from the bowl on the table, and crushed them with her big fingers, right into her soup bowl. I put some noodles into my soup, without crushing them. I liked to watch them float on top, and then push them down into my soup with my spoon. When I put them into my mouth they were all soft and soggy. Momma took the first spoonful, sighed and smiled at me. Then, we both finished our soup, leaving not one drop in our bowls.

After we put some of the sweet sauce on our plates, we neatly cut up the crispy eggrolls with our forks, letting the steam and the vegetables escape while we mixed it all together on our plates, and quickly ate them. I wiped the corner of my lips with the white linen napkin, just like Momma.

The waiter took away the blue and white soup bowls with the white china spoons and the plates from the eggrolls. He brought out two small bowls along with a covered metal container on a pedestal. The bowls each had a scoop of white rice in them. When I put my spoon into the bowl, the rice stuck together in big clumps. I had to push it off the spoon onto my plate with my finger.

Momma lifted the metal cover, and the steam fogged her glasses. Momma and I giggled. With two of the soup spoons, she scooped up one portion for me and one for herself. On top of our chow mein, we put crispy, fried noodles and sweet sauce. Momma took some mustard on a teaspoon, and added it to the mixture on her plate.

I waited while she tasted it. Her eyes filled with tears. As they rolled down her cheeks, Momma took her handkerchief out of her pocketbook and blew her nose.

"Perfect!" she said, smiling at me. Momma ate, cried, and blew her nose some more and said, "That really cleared my sinuses." We both finished everything on our plates.

Now came the best part, the dessert. Momma ordered kumquats with vanilla ice cream. Kumquats were too bitter for me. I ordered plain vanilla ice cream. On top of her ice cream, Momma crushed the fried noodles. I liked that taste, so I did it too.

Momma put the green paper parasol that came with her ice cream in her big pocketbook. I took my pink paper parasol, and put it in my little purse.

By now we had finished all our tea, and a lady came to our booth.

"May I read your tea leaves?"

"Yes," said Momma.

The lady pulled up a chair to our booth, turned our teacups upside down to empty the last drops and then studied the pictures that the leaves formed.

I looked in my teacup. I thought I could see hats, and little dogs, and lots of other things but I didn't know what they meant. The lady did. She could read the tea leaves. She started with Momma's cup.

"Oh," she said, with a serious look in her eyes, "I see tears..."

FIVE

CHESTS ON FIRE

Chicken and soup with lots of vegetables, or brisket, or stuffed cabbage, or borscht with boiled potatoes were always cooking in Momma's big white enamel pots. I loved all Momma's dishes, but my favorite was the baked potatoes. I watched her scoop out the hot white insides, and mash them with lots of butter, milk, and salt. Then to make them really nutritious for us, Momma mixed in spinach, and packed it all back inside the skins. She called these "potato boats." Everything Momma made was so delicious; Lillian and I never had to be told about the starving children in Europe.

Momma took very good care of us. She made sure that we were always clean, got lots of rest, ate well, and dressed warm enough when it was cold outside.

I wore cotton lisle stockings held up by a garter belt. The stockings were a khaki color, constantly drooping and always made me feel itchy. Over these came the pink long-legged bloomers, made of cotton, but called woolies. Once my bottom half was protected, it was time for the top.

An undershirt with sleeves was nice and warm, but not as far as Momma was concerned. She always said, "No winter winds will get to my baby." So, over the sleeved undershirt, I had to wear a sleeveless undershirt, and then of course my blouse, skirt and those ugly laced oxfords.

We lived on the top floor, and Momma spent a lot

of time on the roof. When President Roosevelt came to Brooklyn to make a speech at Ebbets Field, there were Secret Service Men up there and Momma made hot coffee and brought it to them.

She posed the family for photographs on the roof, hung her laundry to dry on the big clothes line, and stood there on school days, and watched as I crossed the street to get to P.S. 241. When I was safely on the other side, I looked up and waved to Momma standing there. She smiled at me and waved back. It felt good being watched over, and I never questioned what she did, until one day in school.

It was chest x-ray day. The girls and I were standing behind the curtain on the stage in the auditorium. We had to take off our blouses and line up in front of the white-coated doctor and his machine, so he could make sure that we didn't have tuberculosis.

My friends and I giggled, as we tried to imagine the boys on their line in the gym. Suddenly the doctor shouted for all the world to hear.

"You there. We haven't got all day. You're next."

I hadn't realized he was speaking to me until my friend poked me.

"Yes, you," he said when I turned toward him. "The girl with the two undershirts."

When I got home from school, I told Momma what happened.

"I was so embarrassed. All day long they kept teasing me. 'There she goes,' they said. 'The girl with the two undershirts,' they said, pointing at me and laughing. Even the boys started saying it. After a while, all someone had to do was hold up two fingers, and everyone got hysterical. I thought I'd die. I don't know how I'm ever going to go back to school. They'll never let me forget it, Momma. No matter what you say, I'm never going to wear them again."

Even two undershirts didn't keep me from getting sick. But, Momma had her own remedies for getting her children well, particularly from chest colds. In the name of love, and with lots of hugs and kisses she set our chests on fire.

Momma cut some wide strips from an old, bleached sheet, and arranged them on the kitchen table. Then she took the box of dry mustard, the hot kind that could clear your sinuses, down from the cabinet over the sink. She measured out just the right amount into her big glass bowl. Adding water, she mixed it until it became a lumpy paste.

She put some of her "magic" yellow filling on each of the pieces of sheet, spreading it out with the back of the spoon, making sure it was evenly distributed. She neatly covered the filling with one side of the rectangle, and then the other, finally tucking in the short ends carefully, so nothing would spill out.

When she was finished, she placed two mustard packs on a tray and marched into the bedroom. She put the tray on the night table, and smiled at me in bed.

"How do you feel, sweetie?"

"Not so good, Momma."

"Don't you worry. I'm going to make it all better," Momma said brushing the hair off my forehead, kissing me with her cool lips.

She unbuttoned the top of my pajamas, and put one of her homemade mustard packs on my chest. After a few seconds, I complained that my chest was burning.

"I know, Flori." Momma said. "It's drawing out all the bad germs."

As I was about to protest again, Momma lifted me up gently, and slipped another one on my back before letting me down carefully on the bed. I started to squirm but Momma cautioned me not to move, because she didn't want anything to spill out and stain the bed.

"If any of the germs managed to survive the chicken soup I fed you at supper, now..." Momma said, "they're doomed!"

Later in the evening, Momma made me what she called a "Guggaler-Muggaler." It was hot milk with honey and a lump of butter melting on the top. I loved the sweet taste. It warmed me all over.

By now I could barely keep my eyes open. Momma gave me a big hug, a kiss on both my cheeks, one little one on my nose, tucked me in, and turned out the light. We both knew that in the morning I'd be fine.

SIX

WATCH OUT

Momma untied my braids and let my long hair fall to my shoulders. She said that the sun coming in from the window showed my fine ebony-looking hair to really be a mahogany-brown, which matched the color of my eyes. I loved when Momma talked like that, especially when she was talking about me. She said it had brick-red highlights in it just like her own. Momma brushed and brushed my hair until it looked and felt, she said, as smooth as shimmery silk.

When Momma was finished, she rolled the top of my hair around her fingers and made it into a pompadour fastened in place with bobby pins that she opened with her teeth. Momma was happy and sang along with the radio as she fixed my hair.

"Heigh-Ho, Heigh-Ho.
It's off to work we go.
We work and play..."

Usually Momma sang love songs but I knew this one. It was from that movie Momma took me to, *Snow White and the Seven Dwarfs*, so I joined right in.

"...and sing all day. Heigh-Ho,
Heigh-Ho, Heigh-Ho."

When Momma was sad she would sigh a lot. Lately Momma seemed to be sad and mad most of the time. I didn't understand, and I didn't like it at all. If she was sad and brushing my hair, she'd sigh deeply and press down on my head with her big heavy hands. When she was angry – watch out!

Like the time with Monte. He lived next door to us on the top floor of our apartment house. His mother and grandmother whom he lived with were both tall, blond, tanned and beautiful like Monte. They were very different from our family. Not only were they Swedish, but his mother was divorced, and she wore leg makeup instead of stockings.

Monte and I were playing in the hallway. He took my book and held it over my head. I jumped up and down trying to get it back, but he held it higher. We were both laughing, but Momma walked by and got angry. She picked Monte up by his ear.

"Ow!" Monte screamed. "Put me down. Stop that! Ow!"

Momma ignored his screams, and without letting go of his ear said, "Do you promise to stop picking on Flori?"

"Ow!" he screamed again while I stood to the side, silently watching.

"Do you promise?"

Tearfully, Monte said, "I promise."

Momma said, "I can't hear you."

"I said, 'I promise,'" yelled Monte.

Momma let go of his ear, took the book and smiled at him, as she marched me up the stairs.

Then there was the time when my sister, Lillian went to Daddy's drawer and took out the wooden cigar box that he kept his coin collection in. Momma caught her playing with them and smacked her so hard that Lillian went flying down the foyer.

Momma was very strong.

When she did things like that, I didn't like Momma very much – sometimes I think I almost hated her. I would never tell anyone how I felt. But, from the look on Daddy's face I wonder if he didn't feel the same way.

Daddy couldn't stand to see anyone cry – especially me – I was his baby. Whenever Momma yelled at me, or hit me, or made me cry, Daddy got angry at Momma.

"I'm telling you, Blanche," he'd yell. "Leave her alone. She's only a little girl."

He'd pick me up in his arms, kiss away my tears, and give me a big hug.

"Don't cry," he'd say as I sobbed into his chest. "Momma didn't mean it."

Once, when my friend Anna Marie and I were playing in Daddy's candy store, we disappeared for an hour. We'd gone to Anna Marie's house, where we took off all our clothes and played doctor. We were only three and when we tried to put our clothes back on, we buttoned them all wrong.

Daddy said he hit me because I was gone so long, and he was worried. Another time he hit me because of what I told him.

"See, Daddy," I said, "I went to church with Anna Marie, and she taught me how to get on my knees and pray." When he hit me that time he said, "Flori, Jewish girls don't kneel in church!"

Daddy only hit me those two times, but Momma hit me a lot more than that. Besides, when he hit me, he was worried, but when she did it I never knew why. It didn't make any sense – she never used to do things like that.

SEVEN

THE HAIRCUT

Mr. Charles, who owned the beauty parlor, helped me into the big chair.

"Aren't you pretty," he said. "What's your name?"

"Florence," I answered very quietly.

"That's a nice name, Florence. How old are you?"

"I'm seven years old," I said looking down at the floor.

The striped apron he draped around me was much too big but he carefully tucked and folded it, and stood back to look at the effect. He acted as if I was his most important customer.

"There now, that's better. Let's see," he said as he started to undo my long brown braids, "What kind of a haircut should we give this pretty girl?"

He pressed on the pedal with his foot lifting the chair up as high as it would go.

"Cut it off," Momma said to Mr. Charles.

"Yes, I understand," he said, "but do you have any particular style in mind?"

"Cut it all off."

Mr. Charles started to argue with her, but Momma gave him her look and he stopped. He took his scissors and snipped a few inches off.

"How's that?" he asked smiling at me in the mirror. I knew he wanted me to smile back at him, but I was too unhappy to do it.

"No," said Momma, "Cut it all off."

I sat in the big chair, and the tears rolled down

my cheeks. I just couldn't help it. Mr. Charles looked at me in the mirror. He tried again.

"Maybe just another inch would be enough?"

"No. I told you. Cut it all off. She has dandruff. I've been putting sulfur crème in her hair for over a week. I can't get it under control. I wash all her brushes, combs, and bobby pins in Clorox every day. No matter what I do, the dandruff persists. There is only one answer, take it all off!"

Mr. Charles turned away from the mirror, looked at Momma, and with a resigned shrug of his shoulders, picked up his scissors again.

My whole body shivered. I shut my eyes tight, as he took a large chunk of my hair in his hand. I felt him carefully turn my head first one way, then the other. He kept cutting, and cutting. I bit my lip so I wouldn't scream. My lips were salty from all my tears. He bent my head forward and cut some more. My neck felt naked. Then he lifted my head and started cutting my bangs.

I heard Mr. Charles put down the scissors and I forced myself to open my eyes. Oh my God, I thought. Look at my ears. Only boys wear their hair this short.

Mr. Charles was brushing my neck with a big fat brush and some talcum powder. He slowly peddled me down, lifted me out of the chair, took the apron off, and handed me over to Momma.

I looked down at the large pile of hair around the chair. I'm sorry, Momma, I thought. I'm sorry I got dandruff. I don't know why. You scrubbed it and scrubbed it, and brushed it so hard. I didn't do anything. Why do you get so angry? I looked up at her, but Momma was looking at Mr. Charles.

I don't wanna go to school, I said to myself, knowing there was no way I could say it to Momma. When she was like this, there was no talking to her. They'll all make fun of me, I thought. They'll all laugh. I look like a freak. My ears stick out like Dumbo's. At least he could fly with his. Mine just stick out and don't do anything but make me look ugly. Why Momma? Why?

I put my hand to my head and tried to pull some hair over my ears. My eyes welled up with tears. It's so thin, I thought. I'm almost bald like Daddy. Lillian didn't have dandruff – didn't have her hair cut. I CAN'T GO TO SCHOOL! The words screamed so loud in my head, I was surprised that Mr. Charles and Momma didn't hear them.

"Thank you," Momma said as she paid Mr. Charles, got our coats and buttoned me into mine. My wool hat nearly covered my eyes now when Momma pulled it on over my new haircut.

Momma took my hand in her wide, powerful one. With a triumphant smile on her face, Momma said to no one in particular, "Now we'll get rid of that dandruff."

EIGHT

LAWRENCE

I snuck into my seat, with my hat still on my head. Everyone was so busy talking and getting their books open that no one seemed to notice me. Except for Mrs. Gordon.

"Florence," she said as she turned from the blackboard to face the class, "we don't wear hats in school. Take yours off and put it away."

"But," I said, shivering, "it's very cold in here." Now, every eye was on me.

"Don't be ridiculous. They turned the heat on today, and it's very hot in here. What is the matter with you? This is not like you, Florence. Take your hat off!"

I really began to shiver now, but it had nothing to do with the temperature in the room. I felt so sick I was afraid I was going to throw up. Maybe, I thought, if I do they'll send me home, and then no one would have to see what Momma made Mr. Charles do to my hair.

"You are holding up the whole class, Florence. Please."

I took my hat off, and quickly shoved it into my desk. I clutched at my chopped-off hair. There wasn't even enough to cover my ears and my neck felt naked and cold. When I raised my head, I saw Mrs. Gordon staring at me with her mouth wide open.

"Florence. What happened to your hair?"

I could barely raise my voice above a whisper,

and I could feel my face get beet red. "I got a haircut," I said.

"I can't hear you, Florence. You'll have to speak up."

I don't think I ever remember hating anyone before, but at that moment I really hated Mrs. Gordon. I wished the floor would have opened up and swallowed her.

"I got a haircut," I said, loud enough for the kids in the next classroom to hear.

"Oh," she said.

There wasn't a sound in the room, but I could feel everyone staring at me. After we started doing our work, I heard it. It was low enough so Mrs. Gordon wouldn't hear, but I could.

"Hi, Lawrence," said Eddie, the pimple-faced boy who sits right behind me. "Are you the new boy in class?" Everyone always picked on Eddie, but I never did. Why did he have to do it? Did it just make him feel good, because now I was a member of The Ugly Club too, and he wasn't alone anymore? Then Jane, who was usually the quietest one in the class, began to repeat it, and soon all the boys and girls were saying it – even Lois and Helen, who I thought were my friends.

The whole class started to giggle.

Mrs. Gordon turned around from the blackboard and asked the class what was so funny, and everyone got quiet again. I bit my lip. I wasn't going to let them see me cry. I used to love to go to school, but now I'd never be able to come here again.

After that, every time Mrs. Gordon left the room,

and after class in the hallways, everyone kept saying, like it was a song, "Lawrence, Lawrence. Florence became Lawrence." Or, "Hey, Lawrence. You have to go home and change. Boys don't wear skirts." I kept wishing I could die.

Finally the bell rang. I put my hat back on, wrapped my coat around me without buttoning it, and ran all the way home.

I opened the door to our apartment, sobbing with tears streaming down my face. Momma was at the sink busy wringing the last bit of water out of the sheets she had just washed.

"Hi, Sweetie. How was school?" she asked, without looking up.

When I didn't answer, she turned and looked at me.

"What's the matter?" she asked as she dried her hands.

How could she not know?

"It was the worst day of my life. I wanted to die. You can't make me go back there!"

"What are you talking about?" she asked, as she tried to wipe the tears from my eyes.

I told her how the kids had been so mean to me when Mrs. Gordon made me take off my hat, and how they didn't stop laughing at me, and how ashamed I felt.

"They called me, 'Lawrence'," I wailed. "And then, when I went to the bathroom one of the girls shrieked, 'Oh my God,' and when the other girls asked her what was the matter, she said, 'there's a boy in here.' Then they all got hysterical laughing and started with that sing-song again, 'Florence is Lawrence.' I just ran out of there. I couldn't even stay and pee."

Momma didn't say a word. She looked at me as if I was telling her an interesting story about somebody else.

"It didn't have to be so short! Why did you do this to me, Momma?"

She held a tissue to my nose, and said, "Blow, Flori. You know your dandruff was out of control, and I had no choice, but to..."

"But, Momma," I screamed. "This is the meanest thing you've ever done to me. Now I'll always be that freaky girl whose mother made her get her hair cut off."

"Now, Flori. In a few days, they'll forget all about it," she said, as she hugged me. "Go ahead now, hang up your coat, and put your books away. I'll go get you some milk and cookies."

NINE

LOST BEHIND HER EYES

Monte and I were in my apartment playing checkers. We decided to look in on George. George lived on a rock, in a glass bowl in the bedroom that I shared with Lillian. George was my turtle. The bowl, the rock, a box of turtle food and George had all come home from Woolworth's together a few weeks ago as a gift for my eighth birthday.

Even though I liked George, some days I simply forgot to feed him. Momma always had to remind me.

"Hello, George. Look who's come to play with you."

"How are you?" asked Monte as he held the tiny green turtle in his hand. "Did you miss us while we were at school? We missed you. What did you do today?"

"Nothing much," Monte would say in a deep voice, pretending to be George.

When I was alone with my turtle, he was kind of boring. Monte made up different stories and voices, and then George was fun.

"Nothing much. Just waiting in my bowl. Just waiting for you and Flori."

I loved when Monte did that.

Today something was different. When Monte picked him up George didn't move. Monte poked him, called his name, and banged on his shell. George still didn't move.

"Whaddaya think, Monte? Is he sick?"

Monte shook his head and said, "I think he's dead. My cousin's turtle died, and he looked like that. And he smelled bad too." He put George back on his rock.

"Yuk," I said, trying to look sad, but all I could think as I stuck my nose in the bowl was, boy, does it stink.

"Momma," I yelled, just as Daddy came home for dinner. "Look at George."

Momma walked into the room first.

"What's the matter?"

"I think he's dead," said Monte.

"What's all the fuss about?" asked Daddy.

"George is dead, Daddy," I said

Daddy walked up to the bowl, picked up George, looked at him, turned him upside down, and looked at him some more.

"Yup," he said, "He's dead!" and tossed the turtle out through the open window.

Momma tried to grab Daddy's hand, but it was too late, George was gone.

"He wasn't dead," she shrieked. "I saw his leg move. He was alive."

"Take it easy, Blanche," Daddy said. "What are you carrying on about? It was only a turtle, and he was dead."

"He was alive! He was alive!" Momma wailed over and over again.

The screaming really frightened me. I was pretty sure that George was dead too, but nothing anyone said would calm down Momma.

"Monte," Daddy said, "I think you'd better go home now."

I walked Monte to the door. We didn't say a word to each other, but when we got to the door, I could still hear Momma shouting at Daddy.

Later that night, when I was in bed, I heard Momma say to Daddy, "I want to go home, Abe. I want to go home to my family in Canada."

I could barely make out Daddy's voice, but he must have asked her, "When?" because Momma yelled at him, "Right away! Give me the money for the train. I want to go home, Abe. I haven't seen them in so long."

After that I couldn't make out the words, and eventually, fell asleep. In the morning, Momma and her suitcase were gone.

"Where's Momma?"

"Oh, she went to visit Grandma and Grandpa in Canada for a few days. Sit down, Flori, and eat your breakfast, you'll be late for school."

Three days later, I was in my father's candy store, after school, reading a Little Orphan Annie comic book. The telephone rang in the phone booth in the back of the store. Daddy answered it, and I knew from the look on his face that something was wrong.

"I don't understand, Moe," he was saying. "What do you mean 'disappeared'?"

Moe was Momma's brother in Canada. Uncle Moe had never called before. What was wrong? Who disappeared?

"What about her clothes?" Daddy shouted into

the phone. No clothes? Who wouldn't want to disappear, I thought, if she didn't have any clothes?

"No, Moe," he said. "Don't call the police. Let me go home and check."

Why would Daddy go home – in the middle of the day? Who were they talking about?

"Of course, I'll let you know," he said as he slammed down the phone.

Daddy tore off his apron, turned off all the lights, put the "CLOSED" sign on the door, grabbed my hand without a word to me, locked the door, and almost dragged me the whole six blocks home, refusing to answer any of my questions. My stomach felt funny.

We ran up the four flights of stairs. Daddy unlocked the door to the apartment. There was Momma standing at the stove in front of her big white enamel pots, with delicious smells coming out of them, as if she had never left.

"Momma. You're here."

"Flori," Daddy said. "Go next door and play with Monte." He shoved me out the door, and slammed it behind him. Even with the door closed, I could hear him yelling.

"Blanche, what's the matter with you? Are you crazy? Moe called. They were scared half out of their minds. You left your clothes and your suitcase. You didn't say 'Goodbye' to anyone. Blanche, answer me. What's the matter? Blanche! I'm talking to you..."

I stood on the other side of the door and listened. Momma never said a word.

Why was Daddy yelling at her? She was home.

Momma was home. Why was he so upset?

Just then I remembered what had made me feel so uncomfortable. Something was strange about Momma – something I had seen before Daddy closed the door.

Momma's eyes had turned towards me when I called her name, but it was as if she didn't see me even though she looked straight at me. What was going on? Did something happen to her? I always went to Momma when I didn't understand something, but I realized that I couldn't today. Momma was lost – lost behind her eyes.

My stomach started to feel funny again.

TEN

THE BLACK REFRIGERATOR

To get to our apartment you had to walk up four long flights of stairs. Most people arrived at the door completely out of breath. The apartment door opened into a long narrow hallway. To the left of the hallway was the room I shared with Lillian. To the right was the bathroom and our parents' room. In the center, opposite the outside door, was the kitchen. There was no living room. The kitchen was the true center – the center of the apartment and of our lives.

The kitchen was decorated just like everyone else's. But, Momma decided to change it. First, over Daddy's objections, she bought a bright yellow table and four yellow chairs with chrome legs.

One day, soon after it was delivered, I came home from school and couldn't believe what I saw.

The table and three chairs were pushed to one side of the room. They were covered with old newspapers, just like the white stove and refrigerator, next to the sink on the opposite wall. The white sink, perched on two long legs, with its one deep side, mostly used to wash laundry, now held two paint cans one opened and one closed, as well as some paint brushes.

Momma, dressed in an old housedress, with a kerchief on her head, was standing on the fourth chair, right next to the sink. All the walls and the ceiling were painted green. She had a paint brush in her hand and splatters of paint all over herself. She turned to me and gave me a great big grin.

"Hi, Sweetiepuss. Don't touch anything. It's still wet. Whaddaya think? Isn't it glorious? No more white kitchen."

"But, Momma. That's the color they're supposed to be."

"All dull and boring. But not ours. Isn't this the most perfect shade of apple green you've ever seen?"

Momma finished painting the last corner. She dropped the dirty brush in the sink, and came down off the chair to admire her work. "There. All done."

"Momma. Why did you...?"

"It's beautiful – just beautiful. Don't you see, Flori? I'm so tired of nothing ever changing. I can't stand it anymore. Everything – so dull and boring..." Momma stopped talking and hurriedly took the newspapers off, uncovering the table and chairs. "Look! See how great the yellow looks against the green walls. Don't you love it?"

"I don't know, Momma..."

"Look at the chrome trim, Flori. My God – It sparkles!" She crouched down and polished the leg of the table with the bottom of her dress. "It's like a mirror. You can see the green reflected in it." She pointed to the window. "Can't you just picture it? I'll make pink curtains, and I'll get a pink metal kool-aide pitcher with glasses and put them on a black lacquered tray. And the best part – I've left the best part for last. I'm going to paint the refrigerator black."

I was glad to see Momma so happy, and the colors

were pretty – but a black refrigerator?

"It'll be so exciting. All those jewel-like colors. I'm even going to use enamel for the black. Everything is going to shine." Momma was beaming. "The colors will define each object. It will make them individual and separate – not washed out in sameness, nothingness, and dullness. They'll be alive!"

"What'll Daddy say? You know how he gets, when anything is different."

Momma stopped smiling. She looked like a balloon, with some of its air leaking out.

"Abe'll see...how the kitchen needed...how I needed...he'll see the colors. He'll..." Nervously twisting her wedding ring on her finger, and biting her lower lip, Momma lowered herself onto the yellow chair.

"Are you all right, Momma? What's the matter?"

I stroked Momma's cheeks and hands, over and over again but got no response.

"Let me tell you what happened in school today," I said with tears in my eyes. "Mrs. Aaron said my story was wonderful...Do you hear me? ...She gave me an A and had me read it to the class. Momma? Please don't do this. Look. Here's the paper. An A..."

Suddenly, Momma sat up in her chair, straightened her kerchief, wiped her hands on her dress, and stood up.

"Flori? Are you home already? I didn't hear you come in."

"Don't you remember? I came home..."

"Go do your homework, I have to finish," she said, as she opened the can of black paint, dipped a clean brush in, and started to paint the refrigerator.

Lillian was upset when she came home and saw what had been done, but she didn't say anything. She gave me a funny look and went to hide in our room.

Daddy was **really** upset. He got very angry.

"This is crazy!" he shouted. "Nobody ever did anything like this before. Where do you get these ideas? You've gotta stop. Do you hear me, Blanche? All this crazy stuff has gotta stop!"

I had seen Daddy angry but this was not like before. Even when he stopped yelling, he didn't seem to calm down. His voice was angry, but his face was scared.

After a few days, life settled down to its usual routine, except that Daddy seemed to be watching everything Momma did.

***

About a week later, I ran up the stairs after school, opened the apartment door, and entered the kitchen. On the stove was a big pot of stuffed cabbage that Momma was making for supper. She must have just put the gingersnap cookies on top, because I could see that the tomato sauce was barely beginning to bubble up through them. Momma was standing over the sink with a large bar of laundry soap washing the clothes on the scrubbing board. The smells of good cooking and clean soap mingled in the air.

The breeze from the window made the pink curtains flap back and forth. It was always open, even if only a little bit, because Daddy always said, and Momma agreed, 'If you don't get enough fresh air you can get sick.'

Under my feet, the linoleum that was green with white flecks in it was shiny clean because everything Momma touched was always scrubbed, and re-scrubbed.

Opposite the stove, in the corner, was a floor to ceiling steam pipe. Whenever the heat was on, it made funny gurgling noises. The rest of the wall was taken up with the yellow table and chairs. Sitting on the table against the wall was the brown wooden radio. *Our Gal Sunday* was on.

"The story that asks the question, 'can a young girl from a mining town in the West find happiness as the wife of a wealthy and titled Englishman?'..."

"How was your day, Flori? Sit down and tell me all about it."

"We got a new book of stories. Do you want me to read them to you, when your program is over?"

"Oh, I'd love that. You'll read to me, and I'll finish my work."

Later that night, after Lillian, Momma, and I ate our supper, and Momma was finishing the dishes, the doorbell rang. Lillian ran to open the door. Three people walked into the kitchen: a large man, whose bulging belly strained against the buttons of his policeman's uniform, a tall, stern looking woman in a nurse's uniform, wearing a navy cape, with a white cap perched on her head, and a short, stocky man, dressed all in black, wearing a chauffeur's hat.

Momma wiped her hands on her clean apron,

invited them into her green kitchen, and offered them coffee from her shiny chrome coffeepot cooking on her clean white stove. They sat down at her bright yellow table, and she poured them each a cup, and stirred in some milk and sugar. Then, she sent Lillian to the corner drugstore to use the telephone to call Daddy home from his store, to tell him what he already knew.

A little while later, we heard footsteps on the stairs, then the key in the door, and Daddy walked in. His face was as white as Momma's bleached sheets. She looked up at him, and introduced him to her "guests." The black refrigerator began to whir.

Momma stood up and in a very quiet voice said, "If you think I should go, Abe, then I'll go."

Daddy just stared at the floor.

She untied her apron, and hung it on the hook on the wall near the sink. Without a word from anyone, the driver, nurse, policeman, and Momma walked out of the kitchen, down the long narrow hallway.

ELEVEN

SILENCE

"How was school today, Flori?"

"Okay."

"Just okay?"

"Yeah."

"Are you all right?"

"Yeah! Just leave me alone, Lillian."

"Something's wrong. Are you getting sick?"

"You're starting to sound just like Daddy. I'm not getting sick."

"Well, what is it?"

"I miss Momma. Don't you?"

"How could you ask me a question like that? Of course I do. And, do you think I like having to do all the laundry, and the cooking?"

"No. But you never talk about it."

"If you didn't make such a mess..."

"I'm asking you how you feel."

"It's not easy for me you know."

"Yeah. But I just thought..."

"I have to go to school and take care of my things. Can't you even pick up your clothes? You're no help..."

"I know," I sighed. Lillian and I just sat at the kitchen table for a few minutes without saying a word.

"Lillian?"

"What?"

"When is she coming home?"

"Flori, that's up to the doctors."

"But, I don't understand. What did she do that...?"

"Please, Flori. What do you want from me? Go do your homework." Before I could say another word, she grabbed my arm and said, "Remember! When Daddy gets home, leave him alone. Don't start with all these questions. Don't upset Daddy. He's had enough! Okay?"

"Okay. Now let go of my arm."

I started to go to the bedroom to get my books, when I decided to discuss something else with her. So many questions, so many thoughts kept going through my mind, and I had no one to talk to about them.

"You know what? I feel all mixed up. I miss Momma so much, but..."

"But what?"

"Sometimes I think, now no one will be mean to us, and Daddy won't be upset all the time, and..."

"Flori. That's a terrible thing to say."

"I knew I couldn't talk to you, but I don't care. And, I don't think Daddy will miss her either. He has me to take care of him."

"That's enough, Flori. I don't know where you get all these ideas. Don't say another word, just go do your homework, and don't come out until it's finished."

"But, Lillian..."

Lillian looked like she was going to explode, so I stopped, but it wasn't fair. Lillian and Daddy never wanted to talk about Momma at all.

TWELVE

MELLO ROLLS AND PIERCED EARS

On my birthday, I got permission to leave school with my best friend, Monte, to get the most important supplies for my class party from Daddy.

We walked across Eastern Parkway to Franklin Avenue where Daddy's candy store was. He had twenty-five mello rolls ready for us. Each mello roll was a pre-packaged ice cream in the shape of a cylinder, frozen in a thick paper that you unrolled and pulled off when you dropped the ice cream into the cylinder-shaped sugar cone that came with it.

Daddy packed all of them securely in a big brown paper bag that he handed to me. Then, he turned to Monte.

"Here, Monte. All the big bottles of soda are in this bag with the cups. It's heavy, can you handle it?"

"No problem. I'm very strong," said Monte, rolling up his sleeve to show Daddy his muscle.

"l can see that," Daddy said. "You two better get going or the teacher is going to come looking for you."

"Bye, Daddy. Thank you," I said as I stood on my toes to give him a kiss.

"Bye. Have a good time at your party, and remember to look both ways when you cross the streets, especially Eastern Parkway."

I couldn't wait to get back. I was so proud to bring the mello rolls to class and be in charge of giving them out. After Momma went away to Creedmoor State Hospital, instead of going straight home from school, I went to Daddy's candy store every day, and stayed there until my older sister, Lillian, got home.

Daddy wore dark slacks with white shirts; short sleeved during the summer and long sleeved with a gray wool cardigan in the winter. He had a long wool tweed coat for really cold weather, and that seemed to be the extent of his wardrobe.

"What do I need clothes for?" he'd ask. "Where do I go?"

I loved being with Daddy. He never got mad at me or said no to me like Momma used to. Except when I wanted to have my ears pierced.

"All the girls are having it done. You're being so mean! Why can't I do it?"

Daddy looked at me standing there with my fists clenched, tears trickling down my cheeks. I was so frustrated; I didn't know what to do. He picked me up and placed me on top of the big red metal ice chest. It had "Coca Cola" in big white script letters printed on its side, and was right in the center of the store.

With a twinkle in his green eyes, he asked, "Is that what you really want?"

I saw that he was smiling at me. I started to feel more relaxed. I smiled back at Daddy.

"You want your ears pierced?" he asked, while he opened one side of the chest where the bottles of soda and big chunks of ice were kept.

"You want your ears pierced?" he asked again, as he pulled out the cold, wet ice pick, and held it up to me.

"Put your head down," he said. "Put your head

down, and I'll do it for you!"

I screamed, and jumped down from the ice chest. I couldn't believe it. First Momma changed and went away, and now Daddy was so mean. What was happening? As I ran out the door, Daddy laughed and laughed.

THIRTEEN

GOTTCHA!

Lillian was eight years older than I was. That made her the boss, especially now that Momma wasn't here. She wasn't too happy about all the extra work she had to do, but when it came to bossing me around – she really seemed to enjoy it.

At night in our room, I would be lying in my bed with its blond wood headboard and footboard decorated with painted Mexican figures, and Lillian would lie down on her matching bed. The lamp stood on top of the night table between the two of us. We could both be talking, but when Lillian said, "That's enough talking. Lights out. It's time to go to sleep," there was no way I could get her to change her mind.

On some nights, when I wanted to play instead of sleep, I would pull my blanket back, and try to get to her bed to tickle her. Lillian always heard me coming.

"You'd better not step one foot out of that bed," she'd yell, "or you'll be sorry!"

That usually was enough to scare me. I'd lie down again pulling the blanket way up to my chin, and quickly fall asleep.

Tonight, when she turned the lamp off, the room wasn't dark. The full moon shining in our window lit up the room.

I tried, but I just wasn't sleepy.

"Lilly? Are you up?"

There was no answer from the other bed, but I

knew from the sound of her breathing, that she was awake.

"Lilly?" I called, my voice a little louder. "I'll bet you're up." Still no response, so I tried again.

"Lilly?"

"Be quiet. I'm sleeping."

"Lilly? Do you want to hear a funny story?" Again, no reply. I started to giggle. "Oh my goodness," I said out loud. "It's so quiet. She must be fast asleep. Sh! I'll have to be careful not to wake her!"

I quietly pulled my feet up to my chest very slowly. Soon, they were on top of the blanket. So far, so good, I thought. Just as I turned to put one foot on the floor, the bedspring creaked.

"Don't you dare get out of that bed!" bellowed Lillian. And then, sounding really menacing, added the usual, "...or you'll be sorry!"

I started to pull my foot back, and suddenly I stopped. I asked a question that never occurred to me before.

"And if I do? What are you going to do about it?"

My voice surprised both of us with its strength. To my amazement, she didn't have an answer. I grabbed the opportunity to jump into my sister's bed and I tickled her, and covered her with juicy kisses.

"Gotcha!" I said laughing. Lillian, laughing with me, didn't seem too upset to have lost some of her power.

Blanche and Abe

Flori

Daddy in his candy store

The four of us, 1940

Momma at Brighton Beach

Lillian and Flori

Flori and Lillian visiting Momma at Creedmoor

FOURTEEN

BEST FRIENDS

Not long after Momma left, Lillian graduated from high school. Daddy didn't want Lillian to take a job for the summer, because he thought Momma might come back home and need her. In September, when the doctors told him that she wouldn't be coming home for a long time, Lillian got a job on Wall Street as a teletype operator.

One Saturday, when Monte's mother and grandmother had to go somewhere, Lillian had to work a half-day and Daddy was at his store. Since Daddy couldn't leave Monte and me without adult supervision, he decided that we would walk over to his store, spend some time with him, and then go to the movies.

Before I left for the day, I had one job to do. The garbage had to be put out on the dumbwaiter, which all the apartments used to bring the garbage downstairs. I smiled, remembering how I loved it when Monte and I had used it when I had the chicken pox a few years ago. Even a dumbwaiter was fun, if I shared it with Monte.

Momma hadn't gone away yet, and Daddy had brought home all the latest comic books for me to read after I felt better. Momma didn't want to take a chance that any other child would find them in the garbage and read them. It would be terrible if they got sick too. So, she made a bundle of all the comics I finished, took them to the backyard, and set fire to them.

I hated to feel sick and not be able to go to school. My whole body itched, but I wasn't allowed to scratch, because Momma said if I did, I'd get scars all over like Beverly across the street. Beverly was fat, had big pimples and lots of holes on her face. I didn't want to look like her. But, what I hated most of all, was not seeing Monte. Momma and Monte's mother came up with a plan to use the dumbwaiter that opened into both apartments. I sat wrapped up in my pajamas and robe, all covered with Calamine Lotion, in front of the dumbwaiter. Monte sat in his apartment in front of the opening on his side, and we would talk and make faces at each other.

"Do I look ugly with all these spots?"

"No. Just weird."

"Thanks a lot."

I'll have to remind Monte of that, I thought, as I put the garbage in, and lowered the pulleys that took it down to the basement.

***

On our way to Daddy's candy store, Monte and I met some of the girls from the apartment building on the second-floor landing. I wanted to impress them. I asked Monte to take out his penis and show it to them. He did. He even peed for them, right in the hallway. The girls wanted to see him do it again, but he wouldn't. Anyway, we had to hurry, Daddy was waiting.

Monte and I were wearing matching outfits.

Navy corduroy pants and jackets, with navy wool berets and gloves. We loved wearing them at the same time. Everyone said we looked like we were twins.

When we got to the store, Daddy filled a brown paper bag for each of us with a sandwich and boxes of Raisinettes, Goobers, and Jujubes.

"Have a good time," Daddy said. "Don't forget – come right back when it's over."

We walked over to the Savoy Movie Theater on Bedford Avenue; bought our tickets with the two quarters Daddy had given us and hurried inside. The bright sun outside left us unprepared for the pitch-black darkness, which surrounded us.

Clutching my paper bag with one hand, I held on tight to Monte with the other.

"I can't see anything!" I whispered.

"Just stand still a minute," he whispered back, holding on to my hand as tightly as I held his. "Let your eyes get used to it!"

At that moment, the Matron arrived with her flashlight. She was a big, fat, gray-haired lady; dressed in a white uniform and white laced-up shoes.

"Do you have your tickets?" she hissed at us.

"Here," said Monte, taking my ticket out of my hand, showing both tickets to the matron.

She shined her flashlight on the tickets, and then on us.

"Follow me," she said as she started down the aisle. Dutifully, we followed the white uniform and the beam of light her flashlight made on the carpeted floor.

At the front of the theater, she stopped abruptly and we almost tripped over each other.

"In here. This is the Children's Section. See? There's two empty seats. Now sit still. And remember – no talkin' or you'll have to go home! You 'unnerstand?'"

We nodded our heads and sat down in the seats her beam of light pointed to. I giggled as Monte made a face at the Matron as soon as she turned away from us and started back up the aisle.

Settled in our seats, we took out the peanut butter and jelly sandwiches. On the big screen in front of us a lot of women in bathing suits were lining up for a contest. Next, the newsreel showed Nazi soldiers marching in that funny way. There were some scenes of Adolph Hitler with that stupid looking mustache, talking to a crowd of people. He wasn't really talking. It was more like he was screaming at them. The people held their arms out straight and kept saying, over and over, "Seig Heil, Seig Heil!"

Remembering that funny song, I started to laugh and I sang it to Monte.

"When the Furher says, 'we are the master race,' Then we 'Heil, Heil' right in the Furher's face..."

Monte joined me in the last chorus and together we puckered up our lips, stuck out our tongues and blew, making that loud noise, like someone had farted, then collapsed into hysterical laughter.

The Matron came running down the aisle, flashing her light in our faces.

"If you can't be quiet I'm going to have to separate you two!"

She left, but we could feel her eyes boring a hole in the back of our necks for the longest time.

After the newsreel, we watched a western, some cartoons, the coming attractions, and sang along with the bouncing ball. We touched each other in all kinds of exciting and forbidden places, ate the candy and had a blissful day.

The lights came on for a brief intermission before the showing of the main feature, *Going My Way*, starring Bing Crosby. When the theater darkened again, I put my hand in his.

"Monte?"

"What?"

"I'm glad you're my best friend."

"Me too."

"We'll always be together – won't we?"

"Sure," he said as his eyes turned to the screen.

FIFTEEN

CLEAN

Daddy was busy with his work for the evening. He sat in the green kitchen, and put his lined notebook, his pencil that he had sharpened with a razor blade and all the money from his pockets in front of him on the yellow table. He separated the bills into piles of singles, fives, tens, and twenties. He placed the coins in stacks of pennies, nickels, dimes, quarters, half dollars, and lined them up neatly.

Every day he started a new page in his notebook. At the top of the page, he wrote the date, and the amount of money he started with.

He spent the rest of the evening listing everything he could remember spending that day, down to the last penny. That total, subtracted from the amount of money he started out with, should be exactly what he had in the piles on the table.

If it wasn't, then he went over his list once again to find the error. If none was found, he sat and searched his mind for an expenditure he had missed.

"Maybe I forgot the package of Sen-Sen?" he'd say, as he went over the list once again. When every penny was accounted for – and he wouldn't close the book until it was – he put the amount at the bottom of the page with a double line under it, and headed up the page for the next day. Then, he could put his money away, and get ready for bed.

The coins were put in a white bowl on top of his dresser, and the bills were all facing in one direction, with the singles on top of the pile. He folded them in half, put a rubber band around them, and placed them next to the white bowl – all ready to pick up in the morning when he left for work.

Daddy got up every morning at four o'clock because he liked to have plenty of time to get ready for work. He'd take his bath, put on his fresh clothes that he had laid out the night before, and then he'd make himself hot oatmeal with cream. He put lots of prunes on his cereal. He said it helped him with his stomach. Daddy was always asking Lillian and me if we moved our bowels. He worried a lot about that. He said if we didn't, we'd have to take Milk of Magnesia, or else we wouldn't be cleaned out, and could get sick.

He'd pack his lunch, do the dishes, make his bed, dust his room, straighten the bathroom, and finally go into our room. He had the mop dampened with water, and he'd run it over the wooden floors, to get up all the dust, especially under the beds.

After he woke Lillian, he'd take his lunch, put on his coat, kiss me good-bye while I was still half-asleep in my bed – and leave for work, making sure Lillian locked the door behind him. Lillian's job was to make sure that I was out of bed, before she left for work.

"Flori, it's late."

"I'm up," I said, as I turned over in bed. Fifteen minutes later Lillian looked in and I was sound asleep.

"Flori, you're going to be late!"

"Okay – okay!"

"Let me see your feet on the floor."

"I'm up – I'm up," I said, as I put my feet on the floor. As soon as Lillian walked out of the room, I'd lie down again.

Lillian spent her last half-hour every morning screaming at me and lecturing about how I'd be late and never make it to school, and finally leaving for work, with me up, but Lillian so aggravated, she could barely catch her breath.

I always made her angry. I never hung up my clothes or put away my things. My side of the room was always so sloppy. It was fine for me, but it drove her crazy. I promised to clear it up but she couldn't wait. She usually ended up doing it herself and getting angrier and angrier with me.

Lillian liked everything clean and well taken care of. Her clothes always looked brand new. When our cousin came from Canada, Lillian gave her some of her old clothes to take back with her. The customs officer thought they were brand new and wanted to see the receipts.

Every Sunday, Lillian did her laundry. She rearranged the food in the refrigerator, to take up as little room as possible. The space was needed now for the wet, wrung out clothing that had to be pressed. In there, the wash stayed damp without getting mildewed.

She set up the ironing board, plugged in the iron, and got a small bowl that she filled with water. She needed to be able to sprinkle a few drops on any area that might have dried out.

Wetting her finger on her tongue, she touched it

to the base of the iron. When the iron sputtered, she knew it was hot enough. She took the cold, wet clothing out of the refrigerator, placed it into a wicker basket on the floor next to the ironing board, and began her work.

After she ironed her slips and skirts, she worked on her blouses. She checked each item carefully for any place she might have missed, and when they were all done to her satisfaction, she put everything away.

The ironed skirts and blouses were put on hangers and neatly arranged in the closet. Every hanger faced in the same direction, with enough space between them to keep the clothing from getting creased.

Her slips were folded down both sides, and then, folded in three, to fit perfectly in the drawer. Next to the slips were her underpants, her bras, and her stockings. You could come into the room at any time of the day – any day of the week – open Lillian's drawers, or the closet and nothing would ever be out of place.

On Monday night, when Lillian went to the closet to lay out her clothes for the next day, she stood there and howled.

"My blouse. Where's my striped blouse? Flori? If you took it, I'll kill you!"

"I was late," I cried, trying to get away from her. "I didn't know what else to do."

"What's all the yelling about?"

Daddy's face had that frightened look that he wore so often lately. I hid behind him, sobbing.

Lillian tried to grab at me, but Daddy kept her away.

Lillian's face was beet red and her voice rose hysterically as she glowered at me.

"I worked all day, getting my laundry and ironing done. She – she went out with her friends. She said she'd do hers when she got home."

"I was going to do it, but it was too late."

"Sure," Lillian said, still trying to grab at me. 'I'm too tired,' she said. 'I'll get up early,' she said. 'Do my ironing before I go to school,' she said."

"Can I help it if I overslept? I <u>said</u> I was sorry."

Lillian ran to the dresser, and opened all my dresser drawers. Everything was so messy she almost gave up. But, she found it in the bottom drawer. Her blue striped blouse was shoved underneath a pile of books, papers, and un-ironed clothing that I had thrown in there.

"Daddy! Look at my blouse. She ruined it. Look at the ink on it."

"What ink? Let me see that."

Lillian held the blouse up for Daddy to see.

"That spot is so small you'd need a magnifying glass to find it," I protested.

"It's ruined," Lillian groaned before I could say another word. "I can't take it anymore! I've gotta move out of here."

"Stop it! Stop fighting. I can't stand this craziness. Why do you do this to me? Enough already!"

Daddy put his hand into his pants pocket, and took out some money.

"Calm down, Lillian. Here. You'll go tomorrow

and buy yourself a new blouse."

"But, Daddy..." Lillian complained.

"No more! Flori – tell Lillian you'll never do that again! And you, Lillian, I never want to hear about your leaving home again."

I poked my head out from behind Daddy's back. "I'm sorry, Lillian. I promise. Really! I mean it! I'll never do it again. I'm <u>really</u> sorry. Please don't be mad at me."

"Lillian," Daddy said, as he walked out of the room, "buy yourself an extra-pretty blouse, okay?"

After Momma left, Cora used to come and clean for us. I loved her. Cora always wrapped her warm, full chocolate arms around me when she saw me.

"Child," she'd say. "You sure are pretty."

Lillian liked her too, but Cora was so fat, when she lay down on the floor to scrub our bathroom, she took up the whole room. She really didn't do such a good job.

"I can do it better than Cora, Daddy," Lillian said. "Instead of paying her every week, I'll do the work, and you can give me the money."

Lillian and Daddy always smelled so clean and sweet and talcum-powdery when they kissed me. I hated to take showers. Oh sure, I intended to, but the days were so busy, or I'd get up late.

Once Daddy insisted I go into the bathroom NOW. I didn't want to take a shower then, so I turned on the water, let the room steam up, and took off my clothes. I put on my pajamas and sat down on the toilet until the steam filled the room, and then I came out. Daddy was happy and so was I.

Sometimes when Daddy came home and I wrapped my arms around him and gave him a big kiss, Daddy would whisper in my ear, "Your breath smells." Other times, he'd say, "Your neck is dirty – you have to scrub better." When he saw the hurt look on my face, he'd say, "Would you rather a stranger told you?"

Lillian, and Daddy made sure that I never forgot about all those people who were looking at, or smelling, me. Someday the teacher will say, 'Flori, you have to go home because you smell.'" Daddy and Lillian laughed at that, but I didn't think it was funny. Life was hard for Lillian and Daddy without Momma and I made it so much harder for them. It wasn't easy for me either. Could I help it if I wasn't like them?

SIXTEEN

NINE AND A HALF

I had seen pictures of Daddy before he had started losing his hair and it had been thick and wavy, like Momma's. Lillian's hair was so curly and wavy, it was almost kinky, and she had wanted to have it straightened. My hair was different. It was straight and very fine. And, everyone else was so neat and clean, but I wasn't. Sometimes I didn't think I really belonged in this family.

All the family's important papers were in an old, worn, brown leather folder that Daddy kept in his drawer, hidden beneath his underwear. He had insurance papers, the lease on the apartment, his citizenship papers, birth certificates, Momma and Daddy's marriage license, and lots of business papers in there, all neatly filed and held securely with an elastic band.

I would look through Daddy's file over and over again until I came to my birth certificate, reading every word until I was satisfied that I wasn't adopted. Then I'd put everything back very carefully so that Daddy wouldn't know I'd been in his drawers.

Now, I had something new to worry about. For the last few days when I went to the bathroom, I found thick, brown stains in my underpants. I wanted to die. How was it possible to make in my pants, and not even know I was doing it?

I thought about Jerry Abrams. Last year in school, he made in his pants. The smell in the classroom was unbearable. Everyone but Jerry complained. We knew he did it. He just sat at his desk and stared straight ahead, with a sick look on his face. When all the other kids left the room, Jerry was still sitting there. I wondered how he got home. How did he ever come back to school the next day? I would have killed myself! They never would have gotten me back. Poor Jerry. No one would ever let him forget it.

I was getting sick about it, but there was no one I could tell. One night I had cramps, and hardly slept a wink. I had felt so jumpy the last few days and was having trouble paying attention in school. Thank God it was Saturday and I didn't have to be there this day.

I pulled up my pajama pants, snuck out of the bathroom, into the bedroom, opened the drawer, grabbed a clean pair of underpants, and was on my way back to the bathroom, when Lillian stopped me.

"What are you hiding behind your back? Let me see."

"Nothing," I said, trying to get out of her grip. "Nothing, really! Leave me alone! Ow! Stop it. You're hurting my arm!"

With a look of satisfaction that quickly turned to confusion, Lillian got the underpants away from me.

"I don't understand. Why would you try to hide these?"

I couldn't hold it in anymore, and started to sob hysterically. "I don't know how it happened, Lillian. Don't be mad at me."

"What are you talking about? <u>What</u> happened?

Blow your nose, Flori," she said. "Stop crying. I can't understand what you're saying."

I dragged her into the bathroom, locked the door and showed her the "evidence." Slowly, Lillian began to smile.

"I can't believe you," I said. "You think it's funny. I'll never tell you anything again. I hate you!"

"Don't you know what this means?" she said grinning from ear to ear.

"That's what I've been trying to tell you," I sobbed. "It means that I made in my pants, and have been doing it for the last few days," I shouted at her, trying to hold back my tears. "And, I don't even know I'm doing it."

"Oh, Flori," Lillian said gently, as she put her arms around me. "You didn't do anything wrong – your period has started, that's all."

I couldn't believe what she was saying. "It can't be," I argued. "Momma told me all about periods and how someday I'd get mine. She said it would be a special day when I'd begin to bleed, just like the two of you, but this is thick and brown. Blood is bright red. Are you sure?"

"I'm positive! You're fine."

"Oh Lillian – really? – My period?" I hugged and kissed her, and couldn't stop laughing. "I thought something was wrong with me. I never thought it was my period." I put my arms around my sister, and started to dance around the bathroom with her.

"Stop that!" Lillian yelled, as she laughed with me. She gave me a kotex pad, and a sanitary belt, and showed me how to use them. "Later," she said, "we'll go down to the drugstore and buy you your own."

Suddenly, Lillian got very quiet. "What happened to the underpants from the last few days? I never saw them in the hamper." I could feel my head shrink into my body, as I said, "I hid them in my bottom drawer."

"Oh, my God." moaned Lillian. "In with the clean clothes? I don't believe you. Why didn't you wash them, or tell me?" She ran back to the bedroom, opened the drawer, frantically burrowing through the things, until she found them shoved under everything. Back she ran to the bathroom, put the stopper in the sink, turned the faucets on, put in some soap, and dropped the underpants in to soak.

"Imagine if I hadn't caught you this morning? How could you do something like this? I don't know if I'll ever be able to get the stains out now."

Lillian went on yelling at me for quite a while, but I stopped paying attention to the words. All I cared about was knowing that I wasn't a stupid baby like I thought. I wasn't a baby at all, I was a woman. I had my period, just like Lillian and Momma. I was sure I would never feel happier than I did then.

"She's only nine and a half years old," I overheard Daddy say to Lillian later that night. "That's too young!" he said. "Maybe," Daddy said, "we should take her to a doctor."

"She's fine, Daddy. It is early, but don't worry," Lillian said, "it's okay! Honest."

"I don't know," Daddy said, "Nine and a half years old? I never heard of that before."

Poor Daddy. It had been about a month since Momma left, and he seemed to be more worried about everything than before. Like cooking, for instance. Lillian wanted to cook, but Daddy would only let her make salads or things you could cook on the burners. Dishes like salmon croquettes that she made with canned salmon, an egg, and crushed saltine crackers. Lillian would mix them all together, make round patties with her hands, and then fry them in the big iron frying pan, until they were brown and crispy.

We went out to restaurants a lot. Usually Ben's Deli across the street from Daddy's store, or to Famous Vegetarian Restaurant on Utica Avenue. Daddy was afraid to let Lillian use the oven.

"What if you did something wrong," he said "and it blew up?"

One day a button came off my skirt and I got the metal cookie box that Momma used to keep the needles and thread in. I was going to sew the button back on, but Daddy wouldn't let me.

"Bring it to the tailor," he said. "For a quarter, he'll sew it on, and then you'll know it'll be done right." Daddy was a big believer in "experts." If a bulb went out in a light fixture in the apartment, he'd let the super change it. "If I try to change the bulb myself," he'd say, "I might break something, or even worse, electrocute myself."

I loved my Daddy. He was always hugging me and kissing me, and I was always jumping up on his lap putting my arms around his neck, and covering his face with sloppy kisses. Daddy called me his "kissing bug."

About a week after I got my period, I said to Lillian, "It was cold in my bed last night. Tonight I'm going to sleep with Daddy, and then I can snuggle up to him, and then I won't be cold."

Lillian got a funny look on her face.

"Sit down Flori; I have to explain something to you."

I settled myself on the yellow chair, sat very still, and looked up at her. Lillian's cheeks were bright red.

"Lillian, are you wearing rouge?"

"No. I am not wearing rouge! Will you please be quiet and try to pay attention."

"Okay, I'm listening. There's no reason to get so angry. Go ahead."

"When a girl becomes a woman..." She cleared her throat. "You know, she can have babies?"

"I know that. Momma told me all about how they grow in your belly and when you give birth, your breasts fill with milk, and..."

"Yes. But did she explain how they get in there?"

"What do you mean? She said having a baby was the most wonderful thing that could happen and..."

"But she didn't tell you about what the man does, did she?"

"No. Did she tell you? – what man?"

"Oh, Flori will you just be quiet. Stop asking so many questions. Just listen. You see, the father plants the seed. I mean, without the seed – there is no baby. Do you understand?"

"No, I don't. What do babies have to do with

seeds? How does he plant them? What does he use?"

"A man has a penis."

"I know that. I'm not stupid."

I was thinking of that time at the beach. A man was lying near us on his blanket, and what looked like a big latke had fallen out of his bathing suit. I didn't want to stare, but I couldn't figure out what that was. I'd seen pictures of a penis and two testicles in a book my friend Anna Marie had, but nothing that looked like that.

When I asked Monte, he didn't know what a latke was, so I explained that it was a pancake. Monte was always trying to impress me with big words, so he told me that it was probably the man's scrotum. I didn't understand that but I was too embarrassed to tell Monte that I never heard of that word. Monte opened his pants, showed me his penis, and how he could pee across the room into the toilet.

I never thought of Daddy like that – except for the time when I had to go to the toilet, and Daddy was taking a bath.

"Can't you wait?"

"No, Daddy. I have to go real bad."

"Just a minute, Flori."

"Oh, Daddy, please let me in."

Daddy was lying in the bathtub, and he put a washcloth over himself. I tried not to, but I kept staring at the washcloth. Daddy's face was all red, like Lillian's was now, and he kept telling me to hurry up.

"Flori? Are you listening to me?"

"Yes, Lillian. I am."

"The man puts his penis in the woman's vagina and they make a baby."

Lillian folded the dishtowel she had been twisting in her hands and put it on the dishrack to dry.

"You see, Flori? Because you're a woman now — that's why you can't sleep with Daddy."

"Because Daddy would give me a baby?"

"No, Stupid. Daddy would never do that."

I still didn't understand, what all that had to do with sleeping with Daddy, but I could see that Lillian was annoyed with me. I'll have to ask my friend Anna Marie tomorrow, I thought. Maybe she'd know.

SEVENTEEN

TELLING A STORY

After Momma left, I no longer went home for lunch. The school didn't have a cafeteria. Everyone except my teacher went home. Daddy sent me with a sandwich, and arranged for me to have lunch with my teacher in the empty classroom every day. We ate and talked, and when she did some paper work, I read a book.

On rainy days after school, all the mothers were waiting outside with umbrellas and galoshes to take their children home. I had to take myself home. Daddy bought me lots of umbrellas, but I always lost them. He also bought me Waterman pens for school, and I usually lost those too.

"You know, Flori. I think if your head wasn't attached, you'd probably lose that also."

"Daddy! I don't do it on purpose."

Today was Assembly Day. The girls wore starched white middy blouses with red scarves tied under their big collars and dark navy pleated skirts. The boys dressed in bright white shirts, red ties and dark navy pants.

Assembly began with one of the bigger boys leading the color guard. He marched them up the center aisle of the auditorium and on to the stage. He carried the American flag set into a black holder strapped around his waist. The top of the flag was crowned with a shiny golden eagle. Everyone stood, put their hands over their heart, pledged allegiance to the flag, and sang *God Bless America.*

I was not enjoying Assembly, like I usually did. I was too busy worrying about what I was going to do in my next class. Everyone was to get their turn, and today it was mine. I had nothing prepared. Momma would have helped me with this assignment. We would have talked about it, and Momma would have come up with some idea – she would have made sure that I was prepared. But she couldn't. She was in Creedmoor.

I wasn't nervous about speaking in public. Everyone was always asking me to read aloud, because they said I did it so well, and I liked doing it so much. But today was different.

What a stupid topic. "An unusual place that you have visited." I had never been anywhere unusual in my whole life.

Lillian had gone to the World's Fair with Momma and Daddy, but I was only three then, and they said I was too young to take on that long trip on the subway. They brought home a Heinz pickle teaspoon as a souvenir for me – I still had it in the drawer.

God, I thought, we don't even have a car. The only place I've ever been is downtown Brooklyn to shop in the department stores there, to Radio City and Macy's in Manhattan, or to eat at Dubrow's on the East Side.

"It's your turn, Florence. We're waiting!"

I felt everyone's eyes on me as I straightened my books on my desk. Two kids had been called on before me and I hadn't heard a word either of them said. All I knew was that both of them had gotten up in front of the room with lots of notes, and one had even made a chart for everyone to follow. I had nothing. I got up from my seat and walked to the front of the room.

Oh, Momma, I thought, as I stood there and looked at the floor, and then out at the class, what am I going to do? Please help me. Suddenly, I knew what I'd talk about.

"I'm going to tell you about visiting someone in a mental hospital," I said, clearing my throat. "To get there..." I told the class, "...we had to take the subway from Brooklyn to Queens, and then get on a bus for a long ride."

I remembered when we went to visit Momma, how I had complained about the long trip.

"I hate this bus, Lillian. I'll never make it all the way out there. I'm going to vomit. I know I will."

"No, you won't. You never do. For God's sake, you're twelve years old. Don't think about it, and the feeling will go away." Lillian and Daddy always told me that – If you're upset about something – just stop thinking about it. Maybe it worked for them, but it never did for me.

I heard the rustling of papers, and shuffling of feet in the classroom.

"On the bus," I continued, "I sat next to a little wrinkled old lady. Her hair was all gray and blond and wrapped on top of her head in a round, fat bun that looked like a bagel." The class laughed. I hadn't meant it to be funny, but I always liked to make people laugh.

"Her bagel..." I said, trying to milk the joke,

"...was covered with a black hair net. She had a shabby, black leather pocketbook. You know, like something your mother would have thrown out? And, she kept rubbing her hands together. They were all red and chapped. She rubbed them, like she was washing them, over and over. Then, she poked me. Right in the ribs. She poked me with her bony elbow.

"I have daughters in Creedmoor,' she said, looking at me with a strange smile on her face."

I squinted my eyes and smiled at the class, like the lady did. 'Three of them,' she said, 'and I go every week to visit them.'

"Then, you know what she did?" I asked the class, as if I thought they'd know. "She stopped talking to me, and turned to the tall Negro man sitting on the other side of me, and told him the same thing."

"Florence," my teacher interrupted, "Maybe you can move on and tell us more about what happened once you arrived." I took a deep breath.

"We walked through huge black iron gates onto the grounds. Inside the gates, it was like we were in a park, with lots of green grass, colorful flowers, and tall trees, surrounded by lots of buildings. The buildings were big, like apartment houses, except they had bars on the windows and porches."

The classroom was very quiet now.

"It's nothing like all those stories we've heard. It's more like the movie, *The Snake Pit*. You know the one with Olivia DeHavilland. The patients are not chained up, or treated badly, or anything like that."

I thought about those scenes where the actress

was put in a tub with ice water when she acted up. I wondered if Momma ever had to go into one of those. I had lots of questions like that, but I never asked anyone.

"We had to pull open the heavy door of the building, and walk up three flights of stairs. We knocked at the metal door. A few of the patients looked through the narrow slit of a window in the door. Some smiled, and some made faces at us." I heard the class laugh again.

"We shouted through the door, 'Please! Call the nurse.' The patients on the other side of the door nodded their heads, as if they would do it, but they never moved. We just stood there, and waited, and finally the nurse arrived.

"She shooed the patients away, and peered out at us through the window. When we told her that we were there to visit someone, she took the big metal ring of keys attached to her belt by a chain, found the long skinny key that fit the door, and let us into the dayroom. She was a big woman. Her dark hair, under the stiff white cap, was cut short. She was wearing a starched white uniform, white stockings, and those white sturdy laced shoes with thick rubber soles that nurses wear. Her nails were cut real short, and she didn't have any nail polish on them.

"After we were inside, she took her key and locked the door behind us, so no one could get out until she let them."

I watched the faces of the kids in the class while I talked. They were fascinated.

"The patients don't wear hospital gowns, or

anything like that. They wear regular clothes."

I thought about seeing Momma, in her pink cotton housedress, with her stockings held up with round garters rolled up under her fat knees, shuffling along in those open shoes, coming to us, when we visited her.

Momma had hugged and kissed us, plopped herself down in a brown tweed overstuffed armchair, while Lillian and I had pulled up some gray metal folding bridge chairs and settled ourselves in front of her.

"How are you Sweetiepusses? Dish me all the dirt! Have you been good girls?"

"Yes, Momma."

"That's nice."

There were lots of things I had wanted to tell her, and questions I wanted to ask her, but Lillian warned me that I wasn't to say anything that would upset Momma. So, I said nothing while Lillian told Momma how much she liked her job in Wall Street.

"Go on, Florence," my teacher said. "That's not all, is it?"

I shook my head and continued – it was as if a door had opened, and inside were all these pictures of the people I had seen at Creedmoor – pictures that I didn't even realize I had stored away inside, and now they were all tumbling out.

"There was an old woman in a chair rocking back and forth. She was crying and singing to herself, and there was a young girl – I think she was about sixteen or seventeen. She looked like she could be pretty, if she combed her hair, and put some lipstick on. The navy rayon dress she was wearing was too big for her. There were no shoes on her feet, only white anklets. She was pacing from one end of the room to the other, and kept stopping in the middle of a step, as if she'd heard someone talking to her. She'd listen, shake her head "no" and then continue on.

"The men in the room wore plaid shirts with striped pants, and all kinds of colors and prints that didn't match. Some wore pants that were too small, or too short, or too big, held up by belts with the extra fabric bunched around their waists. A few stood there with their flies half open. All of them stood apart from each other, and they laughed, or talked, or cried, or stared into space."

I thought about what Momma had said: "I keep my dresses under my mattress. That keeps them neat. I sleep with my head on my pocketbook so no one can steal it. I haven't got much room for too many extras."

On the bus ride home, I had tried to speak to Lillian about what I was thinking.

"Why doesn't Momma come home? It's been such a long time. She doesn't seem so sick to me."

"Be quiet, Flori."

"But, Daddy doesn't go to visit Momma anymore. He says it upsets him too much. If I ask him about her, he just tries to change the subject, and you won't talk about her either."

"Flori, please!"

"I try to stop thinking about Momma, but it doesn't work – I still feel bad."

I knew I wasn't going to tell the class about any of that.

"Your time is just about up, Florence."

It felt like I had just begun, but I checked the big clock in the hall and saw that there wouldn't be enough time for anyone else to give a report today. I looked at the class. There wasn't one bored look on anyone's face.

"Then..." I said, "...we went out the gates and back outside, to wait for the bus that would take us to the subway, so we could go home."

I sat down, and the bell rang. My heart was pounding and my face was hot, but I felt good. Daddy had told us not to tell anyone about Momma and where she was. "Maybe," he said, "they wouldn't want to be friends with you." But, I hadn't mentioned Momma. I just said, "Someone."

My teacher stopped me in the hall later that day.

"Florence that was the best report we've had all term. Thank you for sharing that with us. It must have been very difficult for you."

It wasn't hard, I thought. I was just telling a story, only this time it was the truth.

EIGHTEEN

NEVER SHOULD HAVE LET HER GO

"This is my daughter Flori." Daddy said to the conductor. She's only twelve years old. She'll be traveling alone."

I stood there, as the conductor and Daddy smiled at me, feeling my cheeks get red hot. I couldn't believe him. Why would he do this to me?

"My wife's relatives will meet her at the station in Montreal, but I'd feel better if I knew someone was watching out for her."

The conductor took Daddy's outstretched hand and gave him a reassuring smile.

"Of course. It would be my pleasure," he said, patting me gently on the head.

I wished Daddy would just stop treating me like this. I was not a baby any more, but he didn't seem to understand that.

Before I could board the train, I had to listen to Daddy tell me, for the hundredth time, "Remember to be a good girl and do everything your Aunt and Uncle tell you." And then, "Flori, don't forget! If you have any problems, you call me right away and let me know."

"I will, Daddy," I said. "I will. Please don't worry."

"Flori, do you have your money, and..."

"Daddy! Please! I have to go. The train will leave without me!"

We kissed each other goodbye and Daddy hugged me real tight, reluctantly letting me go when we heard the conductor say, "All aboard."

I was so excited and couldn't wait to start my trip. Lillian would take her vacation from work and we would come back home together, but that wouldn't be for a whole month.

Daddy was sending me to Canada for a summer vacation. It was the first time I had ever been away from home. I was going to stay at my Aunt Esther and Uncle Sam's house in St. Agathe, in the Laurentian Mountains. Aunt Esther was one of Momma's sisters.

As the train pulled out of the station, I ran to the ladies' room, and put on the lipstick that I had hidden in my purse. It was Tangee's Fuchsia. I had bought it in Woolworth's.

This was my big chance. All alone. Who knows what would happen, or who would sit next to me on the trip.

I hurried along to my seat and sat down, knowing I looked a lot older than twelve. With the lipstick on, I could probably pass for fifteen or sixteen. My heart was pounding. The seat next to me was empty. People were all over the train, finding their seats. He was bound to show up soon, and we'd have the whole trip to get to know one another. I was lost in my fantasy, and then suddenly...the waiting was over. The seat next to me was filled. I couldn't believe it. My one chance and who sat down next to me? A nun!

When I arrived in Montreal, the whole family was there to greet me.

"You're so pretty," Aunt Esther kept saying, "I can't get over how much you look like Blanche."

Everyone always told me that I looked just like Momma.

The house in St. Agathe was all wooden, and painted a brownish red, like the pictures of big barns that I had seen in some of the books I had read. It was on the side of a large hill, and all the rooms were on one floor, with a screened-in porch that went all around the back of it. The house was surrounded by lots of big leafy trees. It was like being in the middle of the woods. I fell in love with it as soon as I saw it. How would I ever be able to go home to that little apartment in Brooklyn?

Momma and Aunt Esther's parents, Bubbie and Zaida, lived there with Uncle Sam and Aunt Esther and Cousins Ethel and Hymie. Ethel was a few months older than I was and Hymie was fifteen.

I had heard stories of when Zaida was a young sailor in Russia, and met and fell in love with Bubbie, a young, beautiful, gentle girl. He had always treated her like a Queen and expected everyone else to. There were stories of Zaida's strength, his ability to chop down trees with one stroke, crush things in his hands, and the final line of all the stories always was, "When Zaida picks up his hand to hit you, you better run!"

Bubbie may have been a pretty young girl when Zaida met her, but now she was in her early sixties. Her kind eyes smiled out from her wrinkled, fat face, and she wrapped me in her big, soft arms, hugging me to her warm, full bosom. Bubbie and Zaida spoke some English, but mostly Yiddish. I couldn't speak Yiddish, but I understood most of what they said.

When I looked really confused, Ethel translated for me.

Hymie was awkward and shy, but he was very nice. Ethel took me to the screened porch. She showed me the two cots we would sleep on and the old chest of drawers and closet in the hall where I could keep my clothes.

This was a real home, and a real family, and they were all my relatives. I felt like this had always been my home, and l had just come back, after being away for a while. I couldn't believe how comfortable I felt there. I didn't miss Brooklyn at all.

"Let's pretend," said Ethel.

"Pretend what?" I asked.

"Let's pretend that we were twins separated at birth, and now we finally found each other."

I thought that was the most marvelous idea that I'd ever heard. We planned to write to each other every day when I went back home, and Ethel would come to New York and stay in our apartment.

Ethel told me that it got very cold at night in the mountains, when the sun went down, and that's why we needed the big quilted blankets on our beds. But I remembered how hot it had been in our apartment – how the sun baked down on the roof and the only way to catch a breeze was to sit on the fire escape – and I didn't believe her. We lay on our beds and talked and talked, and it got colder, and colder. Ethel fell asleep almost immediately.

I wrapped the blanket tight around me, and looked up at the stars in the sky all around us. I was too excited to sleep and was still awake when Aunt

Esther came to check on us.

I stayed very still and pretended I was asleep like Ethel. My aunt walked on tiptoe, and crept around to our cots. She gave me a kiss on my cheek, made sure that we were tucked in good and tight, walked back into the house and put my suitcase in the bottom of the closet.

"They're asleep," I heard Aunt Esther say. Then I heard Zaida's voice. He sounded like he was crying.

"I should never have let her go to New York to marry Abe."

"Please, Pa."

"I should never have let her go," he moaned. "Blanche was fine when she was here. Look what he did to her. I should never have let her go!"

Why was he blaming Daddy? What did he do? I'll ask Ethel I thought. Maybe she knows.

In the morning, the smell of Bubbie's pancakes woke us up. We rushed to get dressed, eat, and then off to the lake to swim, lie in the sun, and talk about boys. I was so busy having a good time, I forgot all about what I heard the night before.

One day I was in the den, looking for a book to read. I thought I was all alone in the house. Uncle Sam only came up on weekends, and Bubbie, Zaida, Aunt Esther, Ethel and Hymie were all out somewhere.

I was standing by the fireplace, looking through a pile of books on the mantle, when suddenly Zaida came into the room. He sat down in his big rocking chair, and put his hands out to me. I crawled into his huge arms, and nestled there like a baby. Zaida crooned to me, kissed my cheeks, and hugged me to him. He stroked my hair tenderly, and he cried and laughed. I didn't understand most of what he said, but it didn't matter.

Gradually, I became aware that Zaida was lost in a world all his own. He rocked faster and faster, and he said, "My beauty, my little Blanchela, my love." And, over and over again, "My Blanchela, my Blanchela..." His eyes glazed over, and his stroking of my hair took on a frenzy that made me very uncomfortable. I was frightened, but instinctively felt that I mustn't move or say a word. For a minute I thought, maybe he's starting to change like Momma did, and my stomach began to feel a little funny.

But, just as suddenly as it came, the glaze left his eyes and the rocking and stroking relaxed. Zaida smiled down at me and patted my head. He put me down and without a word, went outside and got to work sawing some wood for the fireplace, and I went off to look for Ethel to play with.

NINETEEN

EVERYONE'S TALKING

The doctors at Creedmoor had discussed Momma's case and they felt that she was ready to come home for a visit. But, they said, it was up to the family, and they should talk to each other about it.

Lillian and I thought it was a great idea, but Daddy didn't. He was such a worrier. He told us about what he had read in *The Daily News* or *The Daily Mirror* over the last few years. The articles talked about people who came home from mental hospitals. The newspapers quoted the doctors saying that the patient was fine. Then, according to Daddy, the articles went on to say that, usually in the middle of the night, when everyone was sleeping, the patient got up and killed everyone in the family.

"Momma would never hurt anyone," we kept telling him. "She's not like that!"

Eventually Daddy caved in, and agreed to allow Momma to come home for a weekend visit.

Lillian and I shared one of the twin beds in our room, and Momma had the other one to herself. It was better that way. We had lots of things to speak to Momma about and our talking would only disturb Daddy's sleep. Daddy slept in the big bedroom all alone.

If there were any lulls in the conversation that night, no one ever had a chance to notice. I filled the room with words. I couldn't, and wouldn't stop. I prattled on and on, until Momma looked exhausted.

"Be quiet, Flori, and go to sleep! I'm turning the light out. Good night."

"Okay, Lillian. Good night, Momma. Good night, Lillian."

It was dark in the room, but I soon got used to it. I was on the side of the bed next to Momma's. I could see that Momma was on her back, with her eyes wide open, and she was clutching her blanket tight under her chin.

I didn't want to go to sleep if Momma was still awake. Finally, I saw Momma's eyes close. Gratefully, I closed mine, and fell into an exhausted sleep.

The next morning at breakfast Momma looked tired. She seemed to be off someplace else. She smiled a lot, but I remembered that look in Momma's eyes.

Before Momma went away, I couldn't wait to come home from school. She was always in the kitchen. She was usually cooking or cleaning, but as soon as I arrived, she stopped what she was doing. She wanted to hear everything that happened in school that day. She gave me her undivided attention.

Then, gradually, things had changed. Momma was still in the kitchen waiting for me, and she smiled at me and asked me all the right questions, but it was different. No matter how much I told her, and no matter how interesting, or funny my stories were, no matter how hard I tried, Momma was lost to me, in a place behind her eyes.

I couldn't help myself today; I did what I had

always done. I started to talk. About everything, and about nothing. I wanted to stop. I heard my words, as if they were coming out of someone else's mouth, but I couldn't stop them.

"How do you like this skirt, Momma? See. It's plaid. You like plaid, Momma. You always liked plaid, didn't you? Did you hear the birds, Momma? You know, early this morning? I heard the birds. They were making such a loud noise. You used to say 'Listen to the birds, Flori. They're talking to their family,' and..."

"Flori, it's enough already," Daddy said. "Stop talking. You're giving me a headache."

Lillian looked at the clock and said, "It's almost three o'clock. I think we should get ready."

We put on our coats, walked out of the apartment, locked the door behind us, and walked down the four long flights of stairs, into the lobby of the apartment house, and out the door, to the street. Momma walked between Lillian and me, and Daddy was just a step or two behind us.

At Eastern Parkway, we took the subway train to Utica Avenue, where we went to our favorite restaurant, *Famous Vegetarian*. The plan was that after we finished our meal, we girls would kiss Momma goodbye, get on the subway train to go back home, and Daddy would take Momma on a different one, back to Creedmoor.

Once we were seated in the restaurant, Lillian kept pulling out her chair and trying to straighten her skirt under her; Daddy went to hang up the coats; Momma sat in her chair, staring at the table.

I sat next to Momma, and never took my eyes off her. Momma stared nervously around the room, and then, quickly dropped her gaze back down to her hands on her lap.

Just as Daddy came back to the table, the waiter arrived. He was carrying a basket of freshly baked warm onion rolls, a dish of butter squares sitting on ice cubes, and a glass bowl of pickles, sauerkraut, and pickled tomatoes. The basket, the dish, and the bowl were all filled to the brim.

The waiter put everything on the table. Daddy watched the waiter put them down skillfully, so that all of their contents remained intact.

"It's a miracle," Daddy said to the waiter in amazement. "Nothing spilled on the table, or on any of us!"

"After years of practice, you learn how to handle things and make sure everything stays where you want it."

Daddy and the waiter smiled at each other.

"You folks take your time. I'll be back in a little while and get your orders."

Lillian sat turning the pages of the menu.

"There are so many good things here to eat, Daddy. It's hard for me to decide."

"You always say that. The waiter will be back soon, Lillian. You'd better hurry and make up your mind. What about you, Flori? What are you going to have?"

"I'm going to have my favorite, Protose Steak with mushroom gravy and kasha and varniskes. What do you want, Momma?"

Momma looked at me, but didn't answer.

"Would you like what I'm having, Momma? It's so good. They call it steak, but it's made out of vegetables. Maybe you'd like a bowl of borscht and sour cream? You always liked that."

Still no response.

"Well, Blanche, what **would** you like to eat?"

"I'm not hungry," Momma snapped at Daddy in a loud voice.

"...maybe cheese blintzes?" Daddy asked, never looking up from his menu.

"What the hell do you want from me?"

"Blanche, lower your voice. You're talking so loud – people are staring!"

Momma was standing and yelling. Daddy was looking all around him, as if he expected someone to come over and make her stop. I stopped hearing the words coming out of Momma's mouth. Lillian was pulling on Momma's arm.

"Ma – please!"

Somehow, we got our coats and left the restaurant. Daddy found a taxi driver who agreed to drive them back to Creedmoor State Hospital in Queens. Momma was now in the cab, shrieking at the top of her lungs, using curse words that we never knew Momma knew.

"Blanche! Calm down!"

Daddy was sitting next to Momma and looked like he had shrunk inside his clothes.

The car pulled away from the curb, and I saw Daddy take out his white handkerchief, and mop the perspiration from his pale, frightened face.

Lillian and I were left standing in the middle of a crowd that had formed in the street. As the mass of people started thinning out, I saw one of my Junior High School classmates waving to me.

"Hey, Flori. Did you just get here? Boy! You missed all the excitement. Everyone's talking about it. They just took a crazy lady away in a taxi!"

TWENTY

TELL DADDY

Momma came towards Lillian and me when the nurse called her name in the dayroom. She was glad to see us, but seemed preoccupied, and didn't want to sit down. She chewed on her lip a lot, and picked at her fingernails.

"What did you say?" Momma kept asking us, as she paced back and forth. "I'm sorry. I wasn't paying attention."

"I was saying, that next week is the last week of school and we'll be getting our report cards."

I knew Momma didn't hear a word I said. Lillian looked at Momma, and said nothing. After what seemed like forever, Momma grabbed our hands and held them tight. She lowered her voice, looking into our frightened eyes, and squeezed our hands even tighter.

"You have to promise me. Do you hear me? You have to promise that you'll tell Daddy that he has to come here and talk to the doctors."

"Yes, Momma," Lillian said, "I promise."

I nodded my head in agreement. I was afraid to tell Momma that she was hurting my fingers.

Momma hugged us and started to cry. Lillian said we would have to leave soon.

"Promise," Momma said again, "that you'll tell Daddy that he has to come and get me out of here."

I was glad that Momma had let go of my hands.

"Don't forget – you promised me," Momma said,

while we tried to kiss her goodbye.

"Yes, Momma," we answered in unison, as the nurse unlocked the door and let us out of there.

Outside the building, we looked up at the porch like we always did, but this time, instead of waving at us, and blowing us kisses; Momma was standing there wailing.

"Tell him. Tell him to get me out of here. I've got to get out of here!"

A few weeks later, when we went to visit Momma again, the nurse seemed surprised to see us.

"Oh, didn't they notify you? Your mother isn't here anymore."

In answer to the look of panic on our faces, she quickly added, "Your mother just had a little problem," and directed us to the fifth floor.

As we turned to leave, she called out cheerfully, "Nothing to worry about she'll be back here soon."

"What kind of trouble, Lillian? What do they do on the fifth floor that they don't do on the third floor? I don't understand."

"How do I know? Just be quiet, and go on upstairs."

Lillian looked like she was worried too, but why was she angry with me?

A different nurse unlocked the door, and let us into a different dayroom, but it looked the same as the dayroom where we usually visited Momma. It didn't make any sense to me.

Momma came to us when her name was called, but she wasn't the same. Her dress wasn't buttoned right, she wasn't wearing stockings, just white anklets; her hair wasn't combed, and she looked like she was half-asleep. She walked very slowly, and when we all sat down, she looked at us as if she wasn't sure who we were.

"How are you, Momma? The nurse told us you had some trouble, and..."

Lillian gave me a dirty look, and kicked me under the table we were all sitting at. I had forgotten that I wasn't supposed to ask Momma things like that.

"Is that a new dress, Momma?" Lillian asked. "I don't think I've ever seen it before?" Momma just looked at her. "Should I tell you all about my job?"

"Your job?"

"You know, Momma. I told you. On Wall Street."

"I don't remember. I have trouble remembering a lot of things. What did you say about Wall Street?"

Before Lillian could answer her, Momma stopped looking at us, and stared into space. She acted as if we weren't even there.

"I could tell you about school," I said. "Momma? Do you wanna hear?"

"What?"

"Do you wanna hear about school, Momma?"

"Whose school?"

Lillian stood up suddenly, and took my hand.

"We have to go now, Momma — to catch the bus."

From the look Lillian gave me, I knew not to mention that there was plenty of time until visiting time was over.

"Okay, Sweetiepusses. Thanks for coming," Momma said slowly, as if she were half-asleep. She let us kiss her goodbye, and stayed seated, instead of walking us to the door.

When the nurse unlocked the door, she told us that all patients who had shock treatments were a little vague for a while, but Momma would be fine.

"Do you think the treatments hurt Momma, Lillian?"

"Don't you ever stop asking questions? Didn't you hear the nurse? She said Momma will be fine."

Of course I had heard, but I didn't want to get Lillian mad, and tell her that I didn't believe the nurse. I was afraid that maybe Momma wouldn't be fine, so I just didn't say anything.

We looked up, when we got outside, but Momma wasn't on the porch. I was upset about Momma, but at least she hadn't hurt my fingers like she did the last time we visited her, nor had she asked us why Daddy hadn't gotten her out of there.

TWENTY-ONE

SAVED

I arrived home after school, and let myself in with my key. The quiet of the empty apartment rolled over me like a damp fog.

Nothing there, I thought to myself as I opened the black refrigerator and tried to find something. There was never anything good to eat in this house.

I closed the refrigerator, walked over to the breadbox, took out two slices of bakery rye bread, opened the refrigerator, took out the butter dish, and closed the door again. Now a plate, and a knife. I spread a thick layer of butter on both pieces of bread, and looked around the kitchen trying to decide what kind of a sandwich to make. I took a banana from the bunch in the fruit bowl.

...and you should never put bananas – in the refrigerator.

Every time I saw a banana I heard that jingle in my head.

...No – no no! I'm Chiquita Banana and I've come to say that bananas like to ripen in a special way.

I sliced the fruit and arranged the little round pieces on top of the thick buttered bread, covered it with the other piece and cut the sandwich in half.

My schoolbooks were on the yellow table, where I dropped them when I came in. I pushed them out of the way and sat down at the table, picked up my sandwich, and took a bite. It was sweet, smooth, and creamy. I devoured it in a few bites. I need something else, I said to myself, and poured myself a glass of milk.

I pushed the empty plate and glass away, and sat staring out the window. The pink curtains were flapping in the breeze and it was getting cold sitting in front of the open window, so I closed it. The steam pipe started making noises. It sounded like voices talking to me, but as hard as I tried I couldn't make out the words. To drown out the voices, I turned the radio on loud, opened the cabinet, took out a bag of potato chips, and picked up my geography book, and tried to read.

I looked at the clock, and realized that Lillian would be home from work in a few minutes. Lillian scared so easily. I decided to have some fun with her.

I turned off the radio, put the dishes in the sink and my schoolbooks in my room. I walked back into the kitchen, opened the oven door, and turned the gas on. Then, I sat down and put my head on the kitchen table, and waited.

My sister would be home soon, and she'd "save" me. I felt myself getting sleepy. Just at that moment, I heard footsteps on the stairs, and then the key in the door. Lillian dropped her keys on the floor and screamed.

"Oh, my God!" she cried, as she hurriedly turned off the gas and opened the kitchen window. "Flori, are you all right? Oh, my God," she said again, as she tried to shake me, and get me up from the chair.

"I'm fine," I answered her sleepily. "I only wanted to scare you."

"Are you crazy?" she shrieked "You could have

killed yourself. What is the matter with you?" She flopped down on a kitchen chair, and started to cry. Only then did I get scared. The joke had gotten out of hand.

"Don't cry, Lillian. I'm sorry! I thought you'd think it was funny. Please stop crying. I wasn't trying to kill myself. Honest!"

"I can't believe it," she said. She took out her handkerchief to dry her eyes and blow her nose. "What if I'd come home late? You could have died!" Lillian started to cry all over again.

"I wouldn't have," I explained. "I was watching the clock. If you hadn't come home in another minute or so, I would have gotten up and turned the gas off."

She stared at me like she had never seen me before. Suddenly a look of horror came over her face.

"What will Daddy say when he finds out?"

I felt my stomach drop.

"Oh Lil – please don't tell Daddy. Please!" I begged.

"Promise me, Flori," she said taking a deep breath. "Promise me that you'll never do anything like this again, and I won't tell Daddy. It will be our secret, but you have to promise me."

"I promise, Lillian. I'll do anything you say."

I tried to hug and kiss her but she pushed me away and started out of the room.

"I'm going to change into my housedress. Did you do your homework?"

"No, but I'll do it right now. "

"Good."

"Lillian?"

"What?"

"I'm glad you're home."

TWENTY-TWO

PRIVACY

Supper was finished and Lillian was ready to begin. She had all the dishes soaking in soapy water. This, like every other detail in our lives, was carefully thought out.

It was Lillian's job to scrub the dishes, pots, pans, and cutlery. Then she stacked them in the dish drainer in neat rows on top of the linen towel, which absorbed the excess water. My job was to dry everything, and together, we would put them all away.

Every night the routine was exactly the same. Nothing ever changed.

Lillian was intent on scrubbing them all to make sure not a speck of food remained. She rinsed everything thoroughly, until she was certain that all the soap had been removed.

"I'll be back in a second," I said, like I did every night. "I have to go to the bathroom." Lillian gave me a dirty look. "I really do have to go," I said. "I can't help it!"

As I left the kitchen, I could feel Lillian's eyes burning a hole in my back.

When I got back to the kitchen, as usual, Lillian had dried everything and put it all away.

"Why didn't you wait for me?" I whined. Lillian glared at me. Well, I thought, maybe tomorrow I'll bring her in the bathroom with me. She'll be able to watch what I'm doing, and then she'll believe me.

Tonight, instead of staying in the kitchen, and listening to Lillian, I went into the bedroom. I gave definite instructions to Lillian and Daddy.

"I'm closing the door and I don't want to be disturbed!"

Daddy knocked on the door.

"Flori, what are you doing in there?" he cried as he burst into the room. "It's dark in here. Why don't you turn on the lights?" Daddy was staring at me with that worried look on his face.

"I know it's dark, but I like it like this. I'm not doing anything! I'm just thinking."

"Can't you think with the lights on?"

"Daddy!"

He backed out of the room, shaking his head as he closed the door behind him.

Daddy didn't seem to understand that I wasn't his little girl anymore. I was growing up, and needed some privacy.

***

Years ago, Momma had a wooden chest made to store the blankets in. She had it made out of blond wood to blend with the Monterey furniture and set it right under the window.

There was no cushion on it, but I didn't care. I loved this window-seat. Sitting on it with my knees drawn up, I stared out the window. I watched as the world outside got dark and God turned on the stars in the sky and the people across the way turned on the lights in their apartments. I liked being able to look at them, knowing that they couldn't see me.

I closed the curtain and took the shade off the night table lamp, exposing the naked bulb. I pulled the small chain, turning it on. It always fascinated me to watch the small, fragile insects fly to the bulb's glow. They flew to the light as if they were driven.

I felt uneasy, as I remembered what I used to do.

When Daddy had decided that I was old enough to be left alone in the afternoons, while Lillian was at work, I thought it was a great idea. But, maybe it wasn't. I missed Momma too much when I came home from school, and walked into that empty apartment. I didn't feel like doing my homework, and didn't know what to do with all the time.

I spotted the empty coffee cans that were lined up under the sink. They were used to collect the fat left in the frying pan after cooking, and then placed in the refrigerator for the fat to harden. When the can was full, it was put on the dumbwaiter with the rest of the garbage, and another can was taken from under the sink.

There were so many cans, I knew they would never miss one so I found another use for them. I took empty pages from my notebook, ripped them into small pieces, and stuffed them in the coffee can. Then, I took a book of matches, lit them one match at a time, dropped them into the can, and watched as the flames rose higher and higher. The papers turned to ashes, and before the flames started to die down, I hurriedly ripped up old newspapers and paper napkins to keep the flames alive.

I loved watching the flames get higher and

higher, but just to be on the safe side, I put the can in the sink, so if the fire got out of hand, I could turn the faucet on.

When the fire went out, I opened the window to get the smell out of the kitchen. After the ashes cooled off, I took the can downstairs and buried it in one of the big garbage pails that the super had on the side of the apartment house.

For a while, I did this every day after school. Even though I enjoyed it, I got scared when the flames got higher. I knew it was dangerous, but I couldn't seem to stop. Each time, I promised myself that this would be the last time.

One day, the flames almost got out of hand, but I managed to put them out before they got near the pink curtains. That scared me so much, that I never did that again.

What would have happened if Lillian and Daddy had found out? They were such worriers. Especially Daddy.

"Did you read this article?"

"What article, Daddy?"

"This one," he'd say, holding up the Daily News. "It says two girls were walking home from the bowling alley, and two men drove by in their black car."

It was always a black car.

"They dragged the girls into the car, and drove off with them. The police are still looking for them. It says here they were out after ten o'clock!"

To Daddy, ten o'clock was the witching hour. In his mind, girls were safe until that time, but after ten o'clock, all the evil men went out, looking for girls out alone.

Some days, I took the paper and got rid of all those articles, before he saw them.

"What did you cut out of the paper, Flori?"

"Nothing, Daddy. Just something I needed for a report for school. Nothing important."

It got easier when I started hanging around with Marilyn and Elaine who lived in the building. They were a few years older than I was, but I got along better with them than kids my own age that had to be home right after school. Elaine's mother was sick a lot, and didn't pay attention to what she did, and Marilyn's mother was a widow who had to go to work every day. Now, after school, I usually went to Marilyn's house.

On some weekend nights, if I wanted to stay out a little later than ten o'clock, I'd call home.

"Hello, Daddy. Yes. I'm fine. Marilyn and I just met Charlie. Remember? I told you about him. He's in her class. Yes. That's the one. Well, he's going to take us home. We'll be home by ten thirty."

Daddy wouldn't worry. It was just girls alone, who were in danger. If a nice boy were with her, she'd be safe. He'd protect her from all the bad people out there.

After a while, I became such a good liar that I realized that I did it effortlessly everywhere – when I cut school, or was late at home, or with my friends. It was worth it, because it didn't hurt anyone, and it kept everyone happy.

Elaine had told me that she had touched a guy's

penis.

"You didn't really touch it, did you?"

"Yes, I did, Flori."

"But, on top of his pants, right?"

"No. He opened his zipper, took it out, and put it in my hand."

"Oh," I had said, trying to sound very casual.

It was one thing when they rubbed that hard bulge in their pants against me, through all their clothes, but touch it? The talk frightened and excited me at the same time. I listened, and watched, and pretended that I did all those things too.

I got in trouble sometimes, like the time I heard that joke that I didn't understand, but knew was funny because each time it was repeated, everyone roared.

"Jell-O comes in seven delicious flavors," I said to a guy I met at party. "Can you?"

He looked stunned, and then he laughed, and held me much closer while we danced. I felt great. It really worked, and he paid much more attention to me after that. But, he kept trying to put his hands all over me. What kind of a girl did he think I was?

I thought I'd die when I found out what the joke meant. Boy. Did I have a lot to learn. I made it my business after that, to learn all the words for sex, how they were used, and all the double meanings. I was never going to get caught like that again.

"You've been in there for an hour," Lillian shouted, banging on the door. "It's not fair! It's my room too. I'm warning you. Five minutes more, Flori, and then I'm coming in, whether you like it or not!"

"Why does she do it, Lillian? Is that normal? I've never heard of anyone sitting all alone in the dark. She doesn't do anything. She just sits there. Are you sure she's okay?"

"Daddy, there is nothing wrong with her. She's just a bratty teenager."

"I don't know Lillian, you never did anything like that," he said, unconvinced.

It got quiet again in the kitchen. I put back the shade on the lamp. Lillian would never understand how I felt about watching the bugs fly to the light, and if she found out and told Daddy about it, he'd really think I was crazy.

"Okay, that's it. Your time is up, and I'm coming in." The light from the hallway shone on Lillian's curly brown hair and determined face as she shoved the door open.

"Come in," I said sarcastically, as Lillian turned on the light. "I heard Daddy talking to you. Why does he always think I'm not normal? I don't know what the two of you get so upset about. I just want a little privacy. What's wrong with that?"

TWENTY-THREE

POOR THING

Marilyn and I hurried down the stairs to the subway, and sat down on the bench. We kept looking at our watches as the trains rushed by. We had to wait another half-hour until we could be sure Lillian had left for work, and it was safe to go back home.

This cutting school was not easy! It took a lot of planning. And, all those people who kept getting on and off the trains, what about them? Surely, they had nothing else on their minds but to look at the two girls sitting on the bench, and wonder, why were they here and why weren't they in school? To make sure they wouldn't suspect, Marilyn and I had to be very clever. Actually, it was my idea, but Marilyn went along with it.

It was my job to make it seem like I was trying to convince Marilyn that we should give "her" – the make-believe friend – one more chance.

"Okay, I'm just going to wait for one more train, and if she's not on it – then we'll have to leave."

"I don't know if we should wait," Marilyn said as she looked anxiously at her watch. "We're going to be late for school!"

"How would you like it..." I asked in a voice just loud enough for someone to hear, if they were listening. "...if your friends left without you?"

As each train arrived, and new people got off, we went through the whole routine, over and over again. Now all those people in the train station would understand the reason we were there, and that we were really good girls.

"Okay, Marilyn. We can't wait any longer for her. We'd better leave, or else we'll be late for school."

Walking down the street, we kept checking to make sure that nobody who knew us and would tell on us was there, and then we ran up the stairs, two at a time, hoping none of the neighbors would open their doors.

"I didn't see anyone? Did you, Marilyn?"

"I don't think so," she said, panting from the climb up the four flights of stairs."

I opened the door to our apartment, and locked it behind us, like Daddy had taught me, and then we ran to my room, and fell on the beds, laughing and trying to catch our breath.

We spent the rest of the day, combing and re-combing each other's hair into different hairdos copied from the movie magazines, putting on lipstick and rouge, and even mascara. We took turns posing in front of the mirror.

"How do I look?"

"Oh, Flori – you look fab-u-lous. You look just like Gene Tierney in the movie Laura."

"Honest?"

"Now me. Give me the brush. How's this? Who do I look like?"

"Greer Garson in *Madame Curie*?

"No! I thought I looked more like Betty Grable."

"I don't know, Marilyn, maybe if you brush it more to the side. Here, let me see. Yeah, maybe."

We watched the clock and when it was almost

time for Marilyn to go home, we scrubbed our faces clean and put things away so Lillian wouldn't notice. Marilyn tried to really straighten up, but I told her not to, because if the room was too neat, Lillian would know something was wrong.

I was careful that Lillian and Daddy didn't see the cards that the school sent home to let them know I had cut school. I didn't have my own mailbox key, but that didn't stop me. When Lillian was in the shower, all I had to do was take the mailbox key from her key ring, take out the cards, and get the key back, before she noticed it was missing.

But it caught up with me. I had been late one time too many and with all my cuts from class, I could get detention. I had an idea.

I stood in front of the closet. How about the white cotton peasant blouse with the flowered print skirt? No, I thought, I look too pretty in that. Uh-uh! That might work against me. I fingered another blouse, rejected a few more, and suddenly stopped. The navy dress with the tiny white polka dots. It would be just right!

I stepped into the dress, and put my arms into the short-puffed sleeves. The little covered buttons went right up to the white pique collar. Daddy always smiled when he saw me in this dress.

Maybe a little rouge, I thought, studying my face in the mirror, as I rubbed some on my cheeks. Easy, I said to myself, taking some off with a tissue. Only a little – make it look natural. One more glance in the mirror. That did it. I looked flushed and upset. Good touch! I ran the brush through my hair, letting it fall loose to my shoulders. Maybe not, I thought, and brushed it back from my face. I took a rubber band and twisted my hair into a neat ponytail. Much better, I told my mirror, as I wet my fingers, and smoothed back the stray hairs on the sides.

Practicing my sweet and innocent smile, I took a last look at myself in the full-length mirror.

When I got to the Junior High School, I pushed open the door to the Attendance Office, and looked at the white card in my purse. Detention? Maybe not.

"I have an appointment with Mrs. Hendricks," I said softly, in my most respectful voice. The woman seated behind the reception desk looked up.

"Is your name, Florence?"

"Yes," I answered sweetly.

"Go right in, she's expecting you."

Mrs. Hendricks was seated at her desk, writing something on a paper. Without looking up, she said crossly, "Have a seat. I'll be with you in a minute."

I sat down in the worn, brown leather chair, straightened my skirt carefully, folded my hands primly in my lap, and waited patiently.

Without raising her head, she turned away from me and took out my file from the cabinet behind her desk. As she read the file, her stern face began to soften and I knew that she was reading the part that said that my mother had a nervous breakdown, and was in Creedmoor State Hospital.

Finally she glanced up, and really took a good look at me. From the surprised expression on her face, I knew I had made the right choices.

"Now, Florence," Mrs. Hendricks said, in a voice that was tender and caring. "It seems such a waste, to give someone like you detention. You're certainly not like the girls I see in here day after day. Do you think I could get a promise from you that you'll make a bigger effort to be in class and get there on time from now on?" she asked, as she smiled into my sad, innocent eyes.

TWENTY-FOUR

DOCTOR SHAPIRO

"I read it, Flori."

"You read what, Daddy?"

He was holding it out to me. My stupid little note that I had scribbled the other day.

"I can't believe you did that. You went through the garbage and took out my note? And – you taped it together so you could read it? I can't believe you!"

I thought I was going to be sick.

"Is it true – what you wrote here?"

"Daddy, what a person writes is private. Is what true? I don't even remember <u>what</u> I wrote."

"Here it is, Flori. Read it."

I grabbed the paper from his hand and started to read.

"I'm so disgusted with myself, I'm no good.

I smoke, drink, cut school, and..."

I looked up at him, wishing I could hide under the table. I couldn't stand seeing the pain in his eyes.

"Oh, Daddy, I was exaggerating. Everyone does those things every now and then. What's so terrible about smoking?" I said defensively.

"No," he said. "The last line. Is it true?"

I read from the paper again.

"I wish I had the guts to end it all."

"Daddy," I said quickly, "I was being dramatic. It's nothing, honest!" I tried to calm him down, but it didn't work this time.

"I think this is serious, Flori. I made an

appointment for you with Dr. Shapiro."

"Dr. Shapiro? Who's he?"

"He's the psychiatrist that sees Momma," he said, with his eyes looking at the floor.

"You mean I have to go to Creedmoor?"

"No, he has a private office in Queens, and I made an appointment for Saturday."

"There's nothing wrong with me, I just wrote a silly note!"

"We'll leave that up to Dr. Shapiro," he said, taking the note out of my hand.

How could I have been so stupid? I thought. Why didn't I flush the note down the toilet? I felt my stomach lurch in fear.

All week I tried very hard to make him laugh, but Daddy was too busy being scared.

Finally Saturday arrived. Daddy squeezed a few oranges, poured me a glass of orange juice, scrambled eggs with lox for me, and buttered my warm bialy. When I finished that, he gave me a prune danish, and a tall glass of cold milk to wash it down with. He had been to the bakery before he woke me. He bought the bialys, bagels, and danish, and stopped off and got the morning papers, like he did every weekend. The only difference today was that he didn't let me sleep until I woke up, which was usually somewhere around noon.

I got dressed while he washed the dishes, cleaned up the kitchen, and set the table for Lillian, getting everything ready for her when she woke up. We left her a note to remind her where we went, and quietly

closed the apartment door behind us, trying not to
wake her on her day off.

At Dr. Shapiro's office, Daddy stayed in the
waiting room, and I went into another room with the
doctor. He seemed pleasant enough. He was about
six feet tall, with a shiny bald head. He peered at me
through his glasses, and smiled. He sat down behind
his desk and motioned for me to sit in the maroon
leather armchair facing him.

The room was wood paneled with lots of books on
the shelves, soft green carpeting underfoot, and
thick green drapes at the window. I would have liked
to get closer and see what books he had, but I didn't
think it was such a good idea. The room was very
cozy. So far so good, I thought. He smiled at me
again, and I smiled back. He seemed to be waiting
for me to talk, but he'd have to wait. It wasn't my
idea to come here. Let him ask a question, I thought,
as I settled back in the comfortable chair.

"Tell me something about yourself, Flori."

"What would you like to know?" I answered
politely.

"To begin with, your father said something about
your cutting school. Tell me about that."

"I hate it in Junior High."

He looked at me and smiled.

"That's a simple enough problem to solve."

"Really?"

"Sure. If you don't cut school, and you do all your
work, it seems to me that you can pass all your
subjects, graduate and go on to high school. On the
other hand, if you continue doing what you're doing

you'll have to stay there longer – right? So, what you're doing doesn't make much sense, does it?"

"I guess not."

"Now we know that you don't like school. Tell me, Flori, what do you like?" I hesitated for a second.

"I like being with my friends. And, I like going to the movies. I like to watch movies a lot."

"Yes?"

"And, I like reading and music, just like my mother. I'm a lot like my mother. Everyone says I look just like her. I have a picture of her, when she was my age, and I really do!"

"But," he said very gently, "you're not your mother are you? You're Flori. Looking like someone, and liking the same things they like, doesn't stop you from being you, you know. Do you understand what I'm saying?"

I nodded my head in agreement. Of course I knew that, but somehow, hearing Dr. Shapiro say it gave me a good feeling.

"How about boys? Do you date?"

I took a deep breath.

"Yes."

"Do you pet?"

He must have thought I was really stupid. Of course I had, but I wasn't going to tell him about it.

"Flori? A pretty girl like you? You mean to tell me that you don't neck and pet?"

I knew what he was doing. He couldn't fool me.

"No, I don't."

Dr. Shapiro decided to change the subject.

"Dreams. What about dreams, Flori? Have you

had any lately that you remember?"

"Yes. I had one the other night."

Dr. Shapiro picked up his pencil.

"Tell me about it."

He leaned forward expectantly. I relaxed, and began to tell him about the dream I remembered so vividly.

"I was in the lobby of my apartment house and suddenly, it was as if the lobby had disappeared, and the whole scene that I saw was brown-toned."

"Brown-toned?"

"Yes, brown-toned, like those old postcards, and photographs. I think they call it sepia."

"Yes, I understand," he said, sounding a little annoyed.

"What happened in the dream?"

"Nothing happened in the dream."

"I mean, what did you see?"

"Oh. It was as if the lobby and the world had dropped away, and all I could see was this sepia-toned scene in front of me. I was looking at a great body of water and lots of ships were bouncing up and down on the waves." I sat back and smiled as I remembered the scene. It was just as clear to me as if I were dreaming it then.

"Yes? And then what happened?"

"Nothing."

"Were you alone in the dream?"

"Yes."

"What did you do?" he asked.

"I just watched the ships."

"And that's it?" he asked as he sat back in his

chair. He had been leaning forward, like he was going to hear God-knows what. He was obviously disappointed.

"That's all there was."

He looked at his clock.

"Our time is up for today, Flori."

Daddy jumped up when the door opened, and he looked expectantly at Dr. Shapiro.

"Your daughter is a lovely and bright girl. She seems to be a healthy adolescent. I don't think you have too much to worry about."

Daddy's whole body relaxed, and he shook the doctor's hand gratefully, while I smiled up at both of them.

"I'll want to see Flori maybe one or two times more, and I think that will be enough."

The following week, Dr. Shapiro welcomed me into his office. When we were seated, he asked me about my week, my friends, where I had gone, and what I had done. I told him everything I wanted him to know.

"Did you have any more dreams?"

I felt bad that I couldn't remember any. I wished I had a new one I could give him.

"Well, Flori, did you cut school this week?"

"No."

"Did you do all your homework this week?"

"Yes."

"And, Flori, did you smoke any cigarettes this week?"

"No."

I smiled at him – happy to be able to give him

something – even if they were all lies.

"Our time is up," he said, coming around from behind his desk. "I think we can tell your father that I won't have to see you again. But, remember, Flori, if you ever feel that you want to talk to me again, just tell your father, and we'll set up another appointment."

Going home on the subway, Daddy beamed at me, and I gave him a kiss on his cheek. Thank God, I thought, I don't have to go there again next Saturday, and I can stop all this smiling.

TWENTY-FIVE

QUESTIONS

Lillian and I got off the bus, walked through Creedmoor's big black gates, into Building R, up the three flights and knocked on the door.

Momma was waiting right behind the door when the nurse unlocked it.

"If you want," the nurse said, "you can take your mother out for a walk today. She's been doing quite well lately."

"Would you like that, Momma?" I asked.

"Oh yes. I'll go get my sweater. Wait right here. Don't go away."

The last time we visited Momma she was wearing a sweater that was much too big for her, and it was an ugly shade of green. We had never seen it before.

"Where did you get that, Momma?" I had asked her.

"From the storeroom."

"What's a storeroom?"

"Leave Momma alone," Lillian had said, in that irritated voice of hers. "Why do you always have to ask so many questions?"

"It's all right. That's how she learns," Momma had said, smiling at Lillian. "Now, Flori, ask all the questions you want."

Momma had seemed like her old self, and yet I wasn't sure.

"You said 'storeroom'. What's that?"

"It's a big room filled with lots of clothes – pants, dresses, sweaters, and shoes. You know, all kinds of things like that – for patients who don't have someone to bring them any of their own."

"But, Momma. You have us to bring you things."

"Of course I do, Flori."

That didn't make sense to me. We brought Momma underwear, slips, and dresses – whatever she asked us to bring. She had her own sweater, so why was she wearing that ugly one? But, when Lillian squeezed my arm, I decided not to ask Momma any more questions that day.

Today, Momma was wearing the sweater we bought her. It was a soft shade of gray, which matched Momma's hair. She was only thirty-six when she left, and her hair was a dark shade of brown. That was only a few years ago, but after the hospital gave her shock treatments, Momma's hair turned white.

"Have a nice visit, Blanche," the nurse said to Momma in a warm, friendly voice.

Momma didn't answer. She just watched the nurse unlock the door, like she couldn't wait. When the door closed behind us, she linked an arm through each of our arms and took a deep breath.

"Now, Sweetiepusses," she said, as we walked down the three flights of stairs together. "Dish me all the dirt."

The sun felt warm on my face as we walked out of the building. It was a beautiful spring day, and all around us everything was in bloom. I saw a squirrel dart way up in a tree.

"Remember, Momma?" I asked as we walked toward the store that was a few buildings away on the hospital grounds.

"Remember that squirrel that used to come up on the fire escape to our window?"

Momma looked confused.

"It came to the window every day, and you used to put food on the window sill for it – remember, Momma?" I could see that Momma was trying, but was having difficulty.

"You fed it every day, until one day..." I stopped to see if Momma would finish the story. After a few seconds, I went on, "...until one day it left its droppings on the windowsill, and you got mad and wouldn't feed it again. You remember? Don't you, Momma?"

Momma smiled at me.

"Here we are, girls. Here's the store."

We had stopped at a building that from the outside, looked just like the others, but when we opened the heavy door, we took the stairs down to the basement, and there it was, just like a store back home. It didn't even have bars on the windows.

It had a jukebox, a counter with stools, and a few tables and chairs where we could sit down and order a sandwich, ice cream, or coffee and cake. We could buy almost anything we wanted at this store, like magazines, pencils, or stationery.

"It looks like all the tables are taken. Let's go sit at the counter. Come on girls," Momma said, leading the way.

The woman behind the counter was dressed in a

faded yellow uniform with a white apron that had ruffles around its edges. Her hair was tucked into what looked to me like a shower cap.

"Why does she wear that thing on her hair?"

"Shh," said Lillian, putting her finger to her lips.

"She'll hear you. She wears it..." she whispered, "... to make sure that no hair falls on the food."

I looked again, and noticed the wisps of stringy blond-gray hair that had escaped from the cap around the woman's ears.

"But, Lillian..."

The woman was right in front of us now, wiping the counter with a wet rag. I let that question just end there.

"What'll you ladies have?"

"We're all going to have ice cream. I'll have vanilla. What'll you have, Momma?" asked Lillian.

"Chocolate, please."

"What other flavors do you have?"

"We have pistachio. We have cherry vanilla. We have..."

I sat and listened, and kept shaking my head no, and waited to hear more.

"For God sakes, Flori. We haven't got all day. Order something. The lady has other customers to wait on."

"Okay. Okay. Don't get so upset, Lillian. I guess I'll have chocolate, like Momma."

I chattered away until the ice cream was served. I dug my spoon into the double scoops piled high in the cold metal bowl. I was glad that we all had something to concentrate on for a while and I didn't have to work so hard to think of things to say.

I was the first to finish my ice cream, so I swiveled around on my stool and watched the patients. They were dressed in their cotton housedresses and mismatched pants and shirts that didn't seem to fit right. Some of them danced to the music from the jukebox – men and women together, and some women together – all dancing. Momma sang along with the music.

"Gonna take – a sentimental journey.

Sen-ti-mental journey home.

Got my hat, and got my reservations…"

I loved to hear her sing. Momma seemed so happy when she did. I smiled at Momma, and twirled round and round on my stool.

At one table, I saw an old couple with a patient – a man who looked pretty old himself, probably forty-five. I guessed he was their son. I watched them talk to him and feed him a sandwich. The woman would break off little bite-sized pieces, and feed them to him, one piece at a time. After he'd finish a few bites, the father would take a paper napkin and wipe his son's mouth. Without a word, the man sat and chewed, and drooled, and took in whatever they gave him.

When visiting time was over, Lillian and I walked Momma back to her building, knocked on the door, for the nurse to unlock it and let Momma back in.

"Goodbye, Sweetiepusses. Promise me you'll be good girls."

"We will, Momma."

Momma wasn't nervous or unhappy today, and I was glad that she was doing well. But, she'd been well like this before. I wondered if Momma would ever be well enough to come home.

TWENTY-SIX

MISSING THE BOAT

"Ira says that Barry really likes you."

"I don't know, Marilyn. He seemed nice enough when I met him at your house, but I don't know..."

"Flori, what's the matter with you? He's gorgeous. He has platinum blond hair – and his eyes – they're the bluest blue I've ever seen, and he wants to go out with you."

"Why would he want to go out with me? I'm only fourteen."

"He doesn't know that. He thinks you're sixteen like me. Anyway, you'll be fifteen in three months."

"My father would never let me go out with him. Barry's nineteen. He's too old for me."

"He's got that baby face – remember? You thought he was much younger, too. Your father won't ask you how old he is. If he does, you'll just tell him he's sixteen. Besides, it's only a date. You might not even like each other."

"Yeah? How could I go out? My father always wants me home early. I guess I could tell him that I'm sleeping at your house."

Why not? I thought. I wouldn't exactly be lying to Barry and Daddy – just not telling them a few details. That way, I could do what I wanted, and keep everyone happy.

"Great idea. He wouldn't worry – because he wouldn't know. I'll tell Ira it's okay, and the guys can pick us up at my house."

Marilyn's mother worked late most nights, and Marilyn stayed alone. Her mother liked me, and was always glad to have me keep Marilyn company because she thought I was such a good influence on her daughter.

***

The boys took us for a ride on the Staten Island Ferry. I had never been on a boat before. It was very exciting. I heard the blast of its loud horn and felt the vibrations of the engines beneath my feet. I looked all around, trying to take it all in.

"Let's go up to the top deck."

"Wait for us, Flori."

"Come on. We'll be able to see everything from up there."

As the ferry pulled away from the dock, the cool wind whipped my hair back from my face, and I felt a shiver run through my body.

"Are you cold, Flori?" Barry asked as he put his arm around me.

"A little."

Barry's arm tightened around me as I leaned over to watch the big ship cut through the black waves beneath us. We were very high up, but somehow, with him holding me, I felt safe. I couldn't hear a word he said. The roar of the engines and the wind rushing around me blocked out all other sounds. But I just smiled up at him, and it didn't seem to matter, because he kept beaming at me, and holding me tight.

The ferry docked at Staten Island, but Marilyn and Ira didn't get up. They just sat there while the crew tied the ropes to the pier, and lowered the gangplank.

"Aren't you coming with us?"

"No. Ira and I are going to stay on board until it goes back to New York. Maybe you two should stay with us."

"That seems kind of silly, Marilyn. Why did you come here?"

"Just for the ride, dummy! Don't forget – the ferry leaves to go back in a half-hour. You don't want to be left behind."

"You're such a worry wart."

Barry and I didn't see too much of Staten Island. We just walked and talked. I had so many thoughts stored up. It was wonderful to share them with him. He had a lot to say, too, but no one had listened to me like that in a long time. I didn't notice Barry glance at his watch.

"Oh God."

"What's the matter, Barry?"

"Take my hand, Flori. If we run, we might make it."

We arrived back at the dock, just in time to watch the ferry pull away.

We sat down on a bench and never stopped talking until the next one arrived.

On the ride back, Barry put his arm around me again, and as the ferry pulled into New York, he drew me closer to him, and kissed me. Other boys had kissed me before, but I had never kissed any of them back. None of them had made me feel like this.

We held hands as we walked up the long flight of stairs from the subway station on Eastern Parkway. I noticed that it was a little after midnight. I'd never been out this late. As we got to the top of the stairs, I saw him.

Daddy! He was standing there, with his overcoat and pants tossed on over his pajamas.

"Do you have any idea what time it is? Marilyn called me."

"Why?"

"Why? Because she didn't know what else to do. That's why. Said she lost you – lost you on Staten Island."

"It's not her fault," Barry said. "We missed the ferry and...

Daddy grabbed my hand, ignoring Barry completely.

"I'm sorry. Really sorry. We should have phoned..." Barry called out, as Daddy and I crossed the street. I was afraid to say anything, and too embarrassed to turn around and look at Barry, standing all alone on the corner.

"I've been out of my mind," Daddy yelled. "What kind of a girl goes to Staten Island with a boy, and doesn't tell anyone? Didn't I have enough in my life?"

It was bad enough that Barry had to hear him, but thank God, I thought, no one else was outside at this hour. Finally, at home in the apartment, I got a good look at Daddy. His eyes were bulging out of his head, and his face was beet red.

"Please, Daddy. Calm down! What did I do that was so terrible? We only missed the ferry by two minutes."

Daddy, who only hit me twice in my life, picked up a chair and lifted it in the air, as if he would kill me with it.

"Some day," he shouted. "Some day I'll drop dead in the street, and it'll be your fault!"

When we had come home, Lillian took one look at us, and hid in our bedroom. I opened the door to the pitch-black room, and hoped my sister was asleep. But, no such luck.

"How could you do that? Daddy was hysterical. We..."

"Lillian. Please. I don't want to hear anymore."

"You're so selfish, Flori. Don't you ever think of anyone but yourself?"

I put my hands over my ears.

"I'm not listening to you. Go to sleep and leave me alone."

"Excuse me!" Lillian said, and turned her back to me.

I tossed and turned in my bed. It was hard for me to fall asleep. I kept remembering Barry and his kiss, and then I heard Daddy's voice, shouting at me. "...I'll drop dead and it'll be your fault!"

I didn't know what to do. I felt like I had no choice. If I wanted to be happy, then I had to lie. But, Daddy – I'd never seen him like that before. Oh, Momma. I don't mean to be bad and upset them. What's the matter with me? Momma – Why did you have to go away?

I lay in the dark, and cried silently, so I wouldn't disturb Lillian. Eventually, I fell asleep.

Momma's eyes were like a wild animal's. I had never seen her look like that. Momma's hair was hanging in her eyes, and she was drooling. I watched her walk over to the brick wall and start to climb it. She was clawing her way up to the barbed wire on top. She was drooling and panting, and now she was screaming – "FLORI, FLORI – I'm coming!" I was running...

I woke up with sweat pouring down my body, tears rolling down my cheeks, and my screams still inside, choking me. Lillian was sound asleep, but it didn't matter. I knew I couldn't tell her about the dream.

The following day, I moped about the house. I felt terrible, and didn't know what to do.

When the doorbell to our apartment rang, I went to the door, and looked out the peek-hole. Marilyn was standing there. I unlocked the door and let her in.

"I was so worried. What happened to you? I saw Lillian and your father go out when I looked out my window, so I thought I'd come check. You could have come to tell me that you were okay."

"No I couldn't. I'm not allowed out. Thanks to you! I can't believe you called my father."

"What else could I do, Flori? I had to tell him the truth. I told you not to get off the ferry. When you and Barry didn't come back, Ira and I didn't know what to think. What would you have done?"

"You could have waited a while. We took the next ferry. God, Marilyn! I wish you had waited. My father was nuts. I thought he was going to kill me. And, he said, he was going to drop dead, and it would be my fault. Can you believe it?"

Marilyn got a funny look on her face, and then I realized that Marilyn's father had done just that – dropped dead – and I was sorry I had repeated that to her.

"Your father? I can't imagine him saying such a mean thing to you. He's always so nice. Boy. He must have really been mad. How about me? Is he mad at me?"

"You? No. Why would he be mad at you? He likes you. It's me he'll never trust again. And, Barry – you should have seen his face. He must have thought, I don't know what – seeing my father drag me home like that – I wanna die! He'll never want to see me again. And, even if he did – my father would never let me go out with him. Oh, Marilyn, what am I going to do?"

"What is the matter with you? Your father will get over it. You know how parents are. As for Barry – don't be such a jerk – there are lots of other boys out there."

"I know, I know. But I never met anyone like him before. I feel like I've known him forever. He kissed me, Marilyn. It was the most delicious kiss I've ever had in my whole life, and I kissed him back."

"Did he try anything funny?"

"No. It was nothing like that. We just kissed, and talked, and held hands, and...now, I'll never see him again."

"Wow! What are you going to do?"

"I don't know. This is the worst thing that ever happened to me."

"The worst?"

"Well – almost the worst. Oh, Marilyn. I'm so unhappy. It's almost as bad as when Monte left. I felt so all alone. Remember? He and his family moved away. They went to live with his uncle in California. He wasn't sure of the address, but he said he'd write and give it to me.

"I went to the mailbox every day – for months, but there was nothing. And I never, ever heard from him again. It was as if the earth just swallowed him up, and he was gone. I didn't think I'd ever get over it. And now, Barry. I don't think I could stand it if I lost him too."

For a minute, I thought about Momma, but that was different.

Suddenly, the telephone rang.

"Hello?"

"Flori? It's Barry."

"Barry?" I repeated for Marilyn's benefit. Marilyn grinned from ear to ear, and gave me a hug, while I tried to sound very casual on the phone.

"How are you, Barry?"

"I didn't sleep at all last night. I was so worried about you. I hope it's okay that I called. Ira gave me your number."

"Of course it's okay. Why wouldn't it be?"

"Well, I was afraid your father would answer, and hang up on me. I wouldn't blame him, if he never let me see you again."

"But, it wasn't your fault..."

"Yes, it was. I should have kept track of the time. We should never have missed that ferry. I tried to tell him I was sorry, but he was so angry. I guess he was really worried. I'd like to come over and tell him..."

'Oh, I don't know. I think you'd better wait a while. You know – give him a chance to calm down."

"Flori?"

"Yes?"

"I had a wonderful time last night."

"So did I, Barry. So did I."

Marilyn was sitting at the table, making kissing sounds, and rolling her eyes. I was trying to pay attention to Barry, but Marilyn was not making it easy.

"What did you say, Barry?" I asked, motioning for her to be quiet. "No. Nobody's here. It's just the radio."

"I said, 'will it be okay if I call again next week?'"

"Oh, I'd like that."

"Great. Bye, Flori."

"Bye, Barry."

I hung up, and while Marilyn tried to find out what he'd said, I kept dancing around the room with her.

A few weeks later, when Daddy had calmed down. I told him all about Barry – except his age – and how it wasn't his fault, and how nice he was. It took a lot of convincing, but Daddy finally allowed me to bring him home. Barry apologized to him once again. Daddy liked him, and Lillian did too. Daddy agreed to let us go to the movies, if he promised not to keep me out too late.

We went to see a movie, where Esther Williams did an underwater ballet. It was very beautiful, but I thought, boy – when I go swimming, my hair never stays in place like that, and if I were allowed to wear makeup, it would probably get messed up under all that water.

I didn't see too much of rest of the movie because I had been too busy stealing glances at Barry's long, blond eye lashes, enjoying the feel of his hand holding mine, and, worrying.

I had made a decision. I was going to tell him how old I was. But, what if he didn't want to go out with me when he found out? I'd die if that happened. Lying was something that never bothered me before, but with Barry it was different. I hated not being honest with him.

After the movie, Barry walked me home, and up the four flights to our apartment. I invited him in. I put down my purse and keys on the yellow table, and checked both bedrooms. Daddy and Lillian were sound asleep.

"We have to be quiet, Barry. Everyone's sleeping. Would you like a cold soda?"

"Okay."

I knew he wasn't interested in the drink, and neither was I. I leaned back against the black refrigerator, as Barry wrapped his arms around me. I answered his questioning kiss, by opening my mouth a little wider. He tasted so good, and his breath was clean and sweet.

I heard Daddy snoring. Barry was running his tongue along my gums, and the roof of my mouth. He was pressing his hard body to mine, and I felt my knees getting weak. We were both getting too excited and I tried to move my body away from his.

"Barry. I've got to tell you..."

"Please," he begged.

I let him pull me close, and I kissed him again. I felt his hand under my sweater.

"Don't, Barry – don't," I said weakly. "Please, Barry,"

I moaned as his hand moved under my bra. "Listen, Barry..."

"Flori?" Daddy called out. "Is that you?"

I froze. I heard Daddy's bed creak, as he turned over.

"Do you know what time it is?"

"Yes, Daddy. Barry brought me home, and he was just leaving."

"Okay. It's getting late."

I could visualize Daddy trying to see the clock on his night table, and then having to put on his glasses.

Barry reached out for me again. I tried to pull my bra back down over my breasts.

"Don't, Barry," I whispered. "My father's awake."

He looked so unhappy, that I felt bad for him. I let him kiss me again, and kissed him back.

"You have to go home now, Barry."

"I'm going – I'm going. I'll call you tomorrow. Okay?"

"Okay," I said as I gently pushed him out the front door.

No one had ever made me feel like this before. But, I hadn't told him. I had tried. Well, maybe tomorrow, I told myself, as I turned the lights out, and went to bed.

TWENTY-SEVEN

FINDING FLORI

"Marilyn. I don't know what to do. I think I'm going crazy."

"Gosh, why would you think that, Flori?"

"I keep having terrible dreams."

"Like what?"

"Well, in last night's dream, the police came to my door to tell me that they had found a little girl dressed in a white pinafore. They came to get me, because they knew I had buried her."

"Wow! That is pretty scary, but it doesn't mean you're crazy. Everyone has nightmares."

Of course, I knew that everyone had nightmares, but I had been having so many lately – the one about Momma climbing over the wall, and now this one. And, I've been seeing and hearing strange things in my head. I thought they were memories, but I wasn't sure. In bed that night, I talked to Lillian about it.

"Lillian, do you have any memories from when you were little?"

"Like what?"

"I think I remember hearing someone taking Momma away in the middle of the night, and she was screaming."

Lillian looked stunned.

"You couldn't. You were only about three when Momma went away to Brooklyn State Hospital."

"No one ever told me that Momma went away another time."

"What was the point? Why go over this now?"

"Because of what I'm remembering, Lillian."

"Do you remember Aunt Rosie?"

"Aunt Rosie was Daddy's sister – the one who never got married, and died a long time ago? I've seen pictures of her, but I don't recall anything about her. Why? Should I?"

"She stayed with us, and took care of us, while Momma was away."

"All I remember is hearing Momma let out a blood curdling scream, and it woke me up. I can still hear the sound in my head."

"Oh, my God. Anything else?"

"Yeah. Momma standing at the top of a lot of concrete steps outside a building. You know – like the kind you see outside a courthouse, or something – and we were standing way down at the bottom of the steps. I was very little, and Momma seemed far away."

"That must have been at the hospital, when we went to take her home"

"You mean you don't have any memories from when you were very young, Lillian?"

"I remember some things – not a lot. What difference does it make? Besides, it's getting late. Turn off the light, Flori, and go to sleep."

I lay there in the dark, listening to Lillian's breathing, and I couldn't stop myself from all kinds of thoughts.

The lying, I said to myself. I'm sick of it. I'm sick of telling everyone what they want to hear – so they won't be unhappy, won't be mad at me, won't be scared, won't think I'm crazy, like Momma.

Dr. Shapiro said that even if I look like Momma that doesn't mean I am like Momma. Can I believe him? He was such a jerk. He believed every lie I told him. I don't want to lie anymore. I have to get some sleep or I'll never get up for school. But, if I fall asleep – what'll I dream?

When I cut school, and when I come home late and worry Daddy – all he ever says is, "Didn't I have enough in my life?" Lillian and Daddy say I drive them crazy. I can't help it if I'm not like them. I don't wanna be like them. They're so boring. All they do is worry about not getting germs, and moving your bowels, and ironing clothes. I don't know why I make them so upset. I don't want to. I try to be good and not upset them. Maybe I am crazy like Momma... I don't know...

Well, I guess I'd rather be crazy like Momma, than be like Daddy and Lillian. All they do is work hard and clean. They never have any fun. They never go anywhere, or do anything.

My eyes started to close, in spite of myself, and soon I was fast asleep.

The next day I made a decision. I'd talk to Daddy as soon as he finished supper.

"Daddy, when you took me to Dr. Shapiro? He kept asking me if I had any dreams to tell him. I have dreams, Daddy. I want to tell him about them."

Lillian had begun to wash the dishes. She turned around from the sink, and gave me her "look." I knew that look. It meant, why are you upsetting Daddy? Stop it!

I didn't care how many looks Lillian gave me, I had to do this.

"What kind of dreams, Flori?"

"Don't look so scared, Daddy. I'm fine. I just want to tell him about my dreams. He said if I wanted to...I could come back. He said, 'Just tell your father...' That's what he said. Honest. He said if I wanted to – I could come back and talk to him – I want to talk to him, Daddy."

"You're frightening me, Flori. Why now? What's wrong with you?"

"Nothing. I'm okay. He said it, Daddy. He said I just look like Momma...I'm okay. He said it to me. He told you. I'm okay."

"Are you sure, Flori?"

"Of course I'm sure. Now, if you don't stop looking so sad, I'll make those faces. I'll give you sloppy kisses and I'll tickle you ... I saw that smile ... Everything is going to be okay, Daddy ... honest."

Lillian was almost finished washing the dishes.

"Flori, don't run out of here. The dishes have to be dried and put away."

"Okay. I just have to go to the bathroom, and then..."

"Flori!"

"Don't make such a face, Lillian. I was only kidding."

The next day, Daddy told me that he had called Dr. Shapiro, and we had an appointment with him on Saturday.

"Thank you, Daddy. You'll see, everything is going to be fine."

It was only Wednesday. I didn't know how I'd make it through the rest of the week, but I did.

When Dr. Shapiro closed the door behind him, I sat right down in the chair – even before he got behind his desk.

"What is it, Flori? Your father said you had something to tell me."

"I lied to you. I want to tell you the truth."

"About what?"

"About everything. I don't wanna lie anymore to Barry or anyone...I don't wanna make Daddy and Lillian unhappy anymore. I'm not like them. I'm like Momma...I don't wanna be locked up like her and..."

"That's okay, Flori. It's okay to cry. Here's a tissue."

"... and I had some dreams..."

"Yes, Flori?"

"You know what else?"

"What?"

"Sometimes I'm so busy lying to everyone, that I feel like I'm lost, and I don't know how to find me."

"How does it make you feel?"

"I feel scared."

"Of course you do. But, you don't have to worry. I promise you – we're going to look everywhere – and together, we're going to find Flori."

I didn't know how we were going to do that, but I felt better already.

EPILOGUE

JUNE 2000

Today, for the first time, Momma looks different. Her mouth is wide open, and her tongue is pushed out as far as it can go, but the tip of it is folded behind her bottom lip. She sits in her wheelchair and stares straight ahead.

When I say, "Hi, Ma." She doesn't even look up. I pull up one of the straight-backed chairs and try again. "Ma. It's Florence. Look. It's me." She doesn't move.

She just continues to stare in front of her.

"How are you today? Aren't you going to talk to me? Look at me. I'm Florence. Your daughter, come to visit. It's Flori. Don't you remember we..."

"Why are you bothering me with all these questions?" she finally responds in a strong, angry voice.

"But, Ma..."

She never once looks at me. She just shakes her head and moves her hand, as if to push me away.

"Go home," she says. "Go home to your own life. Stay out of mine. Don't you have anything better to do? Leave me alone. And," she shouts, "stop asking me all these questions!"

"Ma. I came here to see you. You remember me."

She never turns to me. She just keeps shaking her head, and making that motion with her hand.

"Leave me alone."

I feel the tears well up in my eyes. This has never happened before. When I've visited her in the past, sometimes she doesn't know me for a while, but then I talk to her, and eventually I reach her. But today, I can't get through.

"You're very confused. You know, there are lots of different planets out there, and on each planet, there are families that look alike. I just look like your mother. You want the one on the other planet, but it was very nice of you to visit me. I'm sorry – you're not mine. Go home now. Go find your mother, and stop pretending you're my daughter. Do you think you can fool me? Go home to your life, and I'll stay with mine. STOP PESTERING ME!"

"But, Momma..."

Her eyes go blank, and out goes the tongue again. I feel the knot of pain in my throat, as I get up from my chair, walk to the elevator, take it down to the lobby, walk to my car, get in, close the door, and just sit and sob.

I thought that after all these years I had accepted, moved on, knew, understood, didn't need, had grown past, was too healthy now – to be hurt by her. She's an old sick woman, suffering from schizophrenia and dementia as well.

I blow my nose, and try to calm down. She doesn't know if I come to visit her or not. If I'm there every week or every month – she never remembers. I only go, I tell myself, because it's the right thing to do. I only go because I don't want the attendants to think she has no family, or that I'm not a good daughter. I don't want to visit, but Daddy died years ago, and

Lillian lives in Florida with her family. There is no one else to do it. She's my mother, I tell myself, but she means nothing to me. I'm just doing what I have to. I'm shocked, at how much it hurts that she doesn't know me; that she thinks I'm the enemy trying to make her believe that I'm her daughter. She's nobody's Goddamn fool, she tells me. She knows. She knows what's going on.

Oh, Momma. When I lose you behind your eyes, it's like I'm lost too. Doesn't it ever stop hurting – even after all these years?

I drive home, crying all the way. Finally, all sobbed out, I take a deep breath, and feel a sense of peace and freedom, like I haven't felt in a long time.

Momma, I am so grateful. You taught me how to love and listen, and because you always wanted to hear my poems and stories, I keep writing them. You gave me the gift of so much love and attention, that no matter what, I would survive.

There are so many things that have happened in our family. So many things I told you about when you'd ask me to "dish you all the dirt." Sometimes, I didn't know how you would react. Like when I came to you and let you know I got married.

"Oh Flori. I'm so happy for you," you said.

How worried I'd been that you'd be upset and want to know why you weren't invited, but all you did was smile at me and give me a kiss. And when I told you after I gave birth to each of my two sons, you beamed at me with such pride in your eyes.

I was pretty proud too because I thought I could create the perfect family— the one I lost when you walked out the door. But emotionally I was only ten years old in the body of a woman overwhelmed with life. I tried to deaden the fear and pain by drugging myself with food. When I finally gained over ninety pounds, I realized that the food didn't work anymore. I was out of control, my house was out of control, I had no discipline in any area of my life, and was scared that I was going crazy, and would leave my children, the way you did.

So, kicking and screaming all the way, I spent many years in therapy stripping away a lot of the layers I had protected myself with. I started taking responsibility for myself, and I even began to lose weight.

Of course, there were some things I never told you, or if I did, you responded, and then promptly forgot all about them. Daddy remarried and then got a divorce, and Lillian raised two daughters and became a widow. There have been lots of pain and tears since you walked away.

"Is everything all right, Flori?"

"Everything is fine, Momma," I always answer, knowing you're content, and you have nothing to worry about no matter what is really going on.

Therapy helped me understand a lot, but I still couldn't let go of you, Momma. Until today – and you helped me with this, too.

Today I understand that my obsession with finding the missing loops of film is why I couldn't let go. Even therapy couldn't help, but somehow, I thought our game of "Remember" would.

I know now, that I may never find those missing

pieces and that's okay. I can let go, Momma.

My eyes are dry now, and looking in the mirror, I don't see Blanche and I don't see Flori. I'm not you and I'm not a little girl anymore. I see Florence—a strong, slender, sane woman who worked damn hard to become who I am.

I'm not a child anymore, but I've written a new poem for you. Do you wanna hear it?

Picked myself up off the lowdown floor.
Had enough, don't want no more.
No more lying, no more shame
Tired of playing that hiding game.

Locked me out, locked you in,
Looking like you was my only sin.
Goodbye, Momma. Gotta go
I'm not you and I gotta be free.
Goodbye, Momma
Hello to me.

You know what, Momma? My husband and I are still together after all these years and our sons have grown and built lives of their own. I have my own kitchen now.

It's painted white but it's not dull. It has gleaming white lacquered cabinets, with fire engine red, cobalt blue, and marigold yellow accents. It makes me smile, and I hurry home to it. I still get lonely and scared sometimes, but I'm okay. I feel safe here like I did in that kitchen in Brooklyn, in the forties, before you painted the refrigerator black.

ACKNOWLEDGEMENTS

To Sherryl Jaffee, the writer and teacher, who, after reading my short story, *The Black Refrigerator,* encouraged me to keep remembering because she was convinced there was a book in it. And, Viva Knight, my writing coach, who with her patient guidance and insightful questions, helped me polish and complete my memoir.

To my other teachers at the New School, Omega Institute, Gotham Writing School, Adelphi University, Hofstra's Summer Writing Conference, Molloy College, Great Neck Adult Education, Baldwin Adult Education and Ronnie Kreiss who taught classes at her house – who all helped teach me what writing should be.

To Bruce Jed who so tragically left us, but not before he designed and created the wonderful cover for *Momma's Black Refrigerator* and kept working on it, until we were both happy with it.

To Faith Zubasky for typing my handwritten notes years before I had a computer and Liza Krawciw, my computer coach, who patiently worked with me getting this manuscript formatted properly and taught me what I had to know for it to become computer ready for publication.

To my friends and family, who, as busy as they were, took the time to read my manuscript, and to Ellen Pickus and Gloria Raskin, and all the other fellow writers that I worked with. Their support meant so much to me.

To the Sisterhood Book Club at Temple Avodah who listened to my reading some of the chapters and asked for more.

To all the writing groups I attended over the years, for their kind and encouraging criticism during the writing of this book and especially, Barbara Novack, Writer-in-Residence at Molloy College. When I found her writing workshops in Oceanside and Rockville Centre, New York, I knew I didn't need to take anymore classes. I was home, with a wonderful, nurturing teacher and talented writer, and a group of writers who were also talented, who patiently listened to me read chapter after chapter until they had heard all of it. Larry who gave me the final title, Irene, Michelle, Ofelia, Iris, Bruce, Doreen, Sue, Trish, and everyone else in the group who listened to my readings and, in their own intimate writings, shared so much of themselves.

I am so very grateful.

ABOUT THE AUTHOR

FLORENCE TANNEN has written many stories about family relationships.

Her short story, *I'll Never Forget was* printed in an anthology published by Omega Institute. Her memoir, *Momma's Black Refrigerator* is her second full length book. *The Haircut,* an excerpt from this book, was awarded Honorable Mention in the Personal Essay category of the 73rd Annual Writer's Digest Writing Competition. *The Black Refrigerator,* an excerpt from this book, was awarded Fifth Place in the Memoir/Personal Essay category of the 85th Annual Writer's Digest Writing Competition.

She is the mother of two sons and lives with her husband on Long Island, New York, where she is at work on a novel, *Such a Good Girl.*

Recent Releases
From
Casa de Snapdragon

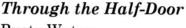

Through the Half-Door
Rusty Watson
ISBN: 978-1-937240-75-2
Genre: Historical fiction/romance

Journey Through the Half-Door is a love story that propels you from the warm experience of cherished love of family and young love to weaving new friendships in a strange new world. It is a chronicle of the emigrants' love of their homeland but respect for their adopted land. The story is the releasing of a lost love as well as the mending qualities of new found love. It is the tale of devastating and unimaginable losses that have painstakingly woven strength of character into the resilient fabric of the main characters' existence. It is the story of my Great-grandmothers' life, a courageous and proud "Irish Bridget."

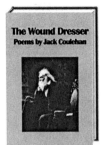

The Wound Dresser
Jack Coulehan
ISBN: 978-1-937240-73-8
Genre: Poetry

The Wound Dresser, Jack Coulehan's sixth collection of poems, explores the mysterious tension between tenderness and steadiness in medical practice. Surprised at his own conflicted feelings about his role as a physician, Coulehan seeks to emulate the tender care shown by Walt Whitman as he comforted wounded Civil War soldiers. In so doing, he discovers the healing power of human contact and engagement. With directness, passion, and often humor, these poems evoke an ethic of compassionate solidarity — between patient and doctor, person and family, the individual and the human community. Robert Pinsky, Poet Laureate of the United States from 1997 to 2000, selected *The Wound Dresser* as a finalist for the 2016 Dorset Poetry Prize.

Grabbing the Apple
Edited by Terri Muuss & M.J. Tenerelli
ISBN: 978-1-937240-70-7
Genre: Poetry

The story of Eve has been, more often than not, interpreted by men. Eve has been presented as impulsive, disobedient and ignorant. But what if Eve were the real hero and mother of us all? Where would we be had she never looked for knowledge, asked the important questions, challenged the powers that be? In this beautiful collection of over 40 New York women poets, the strength, vitality and unique voices of women emerge to answer some of these questions. Energy, savvy, wisdom and power emanate from these poems, both individually and as a collection. The women whose work has been anthologized in this collection are as bold as New York, as brave as Eve. Not content to have their stories told for them, these poets grab the apple with both hands and tell it themselves. *Grabbing the Apple* is a powerful an amazing resource for any reader or student who wants to explore an in-depth selection of work from some of New York's finest and strongest women poets.

CPSIA information can be obtained
at www.ICGtesting.com
Printed in the USA
FFOW05n0003060817

9 781937 240851